D1593492

Raw Frontier:

Armed Conflict Along The Texas Coastal Bend

Volume One

89421

By

Keith Guthrie

EAKIN PRESS ★ Austin, TX

J. M. HODGES LEARNING CENTER
WHARTON COUNTY JUNIOR COLLEGE
WHARTON, TEXAS 77488

FIRST EDITION

Copyright © 1998
By Keith Guthrie

Published in the United States of America
By Eakin Press
A Division of Sunbelt Media, Inc.
P.O. Drawer 90159
Austin, TX 78709

ALL RIGHTS RESERVED.

2 3 4 5 6 7 8 9

ISBN 1-57168-234-1

99-15817

F
392
.C517
G88
1998
C.1

89421

I am indebted to many people who had a part in gathering material for this book. Noted historians like Hobart Huson and Judge Paul Boethel set a high standard for research. The material that they left behind pointed the way to many sources. Researchers like H.P.N. Gammel left a blueprint of the actions of the people who shaped Texas. Hundreds of historians took the time to gather priceless letters, original documents, and memorabilia that revealed the character of our forefathers. These papers are stored in research centers throughout Texas and the custodians are willing to help point the way. All of the historians who have passed before me made my job easier.

JIM HODGES LEARNING CENTER
WHARTON COUNTY JUNIOR COLLEGE
WHARTON, TEXAS 77488

CONTENTS

PREFACE

The name *Raw Frontier* comes from the editors of the *Houston Telegraph and Register.* They used the term frequently to describe Texas' western frontier. To the editors, the area west of the Colorado River was the western frontier, or the Raw Frontier. They ran a column on an almost daily basis entitled "Indian Depredations on the Western Frontier." We have focused on sixteen of these counties for our two books. Volume One is *Raw Frontier: Armed Conflict Along the Texas Coastal Bend.* Volume Two will be *Raw Frontier: Survival to Prosperity on the Texas Coastal Bend.*

Survival on the "Raw Frontier" was multi-faceted. Too often frontier families had to depend on their muzzle-loaded rifles to protect themselves from bandits, Indians, and unscrupulous individuals who were ready with schemes to relieve settlers of their property.

The men and women of this period developed a sense of community that helped them meet these challenges head-on. A neighbor might be one or ten miles distant, but he would come running with his gun if called upon. It was this protective bond that drew communities and individuals together to solve their problems and grow. The bond helped them build schools, churches, and communities. Growth was slow, but as the flood of settlers arrived in Texas during the Republic days seeking to gain title to land that was virtually free for the asking, the Raw Frontier grew as the men and women met, and surmounted, all challenges.

As my wife, Iris, and I traveled extensively in the sixteen-county Raw Frontier, we found that the descendants of these early pioneers were also cooperative and trusting, just like their forebears. As we sat in the home of Mrs. M. K. Dickey in Lolita this trust was evident when she agreed to turn over priceless family documents to us for study. This happened time and time again as we interviewed throughout the area. To these people we owe a debt of gratitude.

Since we live in a small community, I depended a great deal on the South Texas Inter-Library Loan program. Our requests were funneled into Corpus Christi by our local librarian, Mary Griffin, where they were processed. Margaret Rose, in charge of the local history room in the Corpus Christi Public Main Library, helped us in many ways get the books we wanted.

Others loaned us rare books, like Dr. John Tunnell, who shared his Texana collection with us, and attorney John Miller, who allowed us the use of the first couple of volumes of *Gammel Laws*—a must in tracing the growth of communities and counties. Chairmen of historical commissions throughout the area took time to help us locate descendants of pioneer settlers. Newspapers also helped us get our message out to the people we needed to contact.

To all of these fine folks, and the literally scores of others who took time to allow us to interview them, we say, *THANKS*, come see us.

PROLOGUE

Everything must have a beginning; however, the dawn of Texas history is blurry. The Spanish and Mexican land grant period opened colonization in Texas to Anglo settlers in December of 1821 by Empresario Stephen F. Austin. Leading up to this period, Spain, France, and then the United States were competitors for control of the area.

The first Spanish settlements in Texas were constructed in 1690 when Captain Alonso de Leon and Father Damian Massanet set up a mission called San Francisco de los Tejas on the Neches River, about twenty-five miles from present-day Crockett. In 1693 this project was abandoned when the missionaries uncovered an Indian plan to massacre the Spaniards.

In 1699 France began taking possession of the province of Louisiana, which had been claimed for them by La Salle. French traders, working out of Natchitoches around 1713, began sending traders to Indian tribes in present-day Texas, or Spanish territory.

The Spanish were pushing toward the Rio Grande while the French were beginning to control the Mississippi Valley. Father Francisco Hidalgo had continued to push for permission from Spain to reestablish missions in East Texas, without results. Understanding international intrigue, Father Hidalgo wrote a letter to the

French government pointing out to them the trade possibilities in Texas. The French seized the opening and in 1714 Louis Jachereau de Saint Denis was in Natchitoches, the French trading post on the Red River, poised to investigate trade possibilities in Texas.

The Spanish, as a result of Louis Saint Denis's expeditions, authorized Father Hidalgo on July 3, 1716, to reestablish the East Texas missions. By 1717 Spain and France were posturing with missions and trade, trying to win over Indians to their way of thinking. The Indians? They were friendly to the Spanish *padres*, but at the same time they liked trading with the French on the Red River. A French attack in 1719 caused the Spanish to retreat for two years, returning with protection of a hundred soldiers. Eventually, the Spanish friars transferred their activities to the San Antonio River Valley where they were well received.

Spain made still another effort in 1721 when the Marquis de Aguayo led 500 soldiers to firmly plant the Spanish presence in East Texas. About the only lasting good of this effort was the establishment of the Arroyo Hondo, a branch of the Red River, as the boundary between France and Spain. This was the beginning of the neutral zone, or disputed land, between Spain and France and later between Mexico and the United States, and finally with the Republic of Texas and the United States.

French encroachment into Spanish territory ended in 1762 when the territory of Louisiana was transferred from France to Spain. Spain's big worry now was protecting Florida from the flow of settlers from the United States. Life in East Texas became stable as Nacogdoches was founded in 1779. The area prospered.

Spain was apprehensive that the United States would take over part of their territory after their acquisition of the Louisiana Territory from France in the Treaty of 1763. In Louisiana there was an uneasy feeling as Americans crowded westward toward French/Spanish New Orleans.[1]

One of the first American adventurers to draw Spanish attention was Philip Nolan, who pioneered trade with San Antonio from a United States base in Natchez, Miss. He drove wild horses from Texas into New Orleans for a Spanish regiment being organized there. His passport was obtained from the Baron de Carondelet, governor of Louisiana, on July 17, 1797. During an 1800 expedition out of Natchez he was challenged by Spanish troops unsuccessfully.

Nolan's escape was temporary, as he was killed and his men taken prisoner in an engagement that probably occurred in Johnson County on what is now known as Nolan Creek, near the present site of Waco. The attack was led by Lieutenant M. Mazquiz with about one hundred men on March 21, 1801. Nolan's ears were cut off to prove to the governor of Texas that he was indeed dead. Nolan's men were taken captive, some escaped, and the rest remained in Chihuahua, where they were tried by Spanish authorities as invaders. It was ordered that one out of five be hanged. Of the ten prisoners, one died (Joseph Pierce) and the authorities decided that only one man had to be hanged. The men threw dice, with the low man to die. Ephraim Blackburn threw a three and one and was hanged November 11, 1807.[2]

The United States became an official neighbor of Spain in 1803 through the Louisiana Purchase. In 1800 Napoleon Bonaparte, in a bid to revive the French Empire in America, had required of Spain the retrocession of Louisiana. Pres. Jefferson Davis coveted the territory and a deal was worked whereby the entire Louisiana Territory was acquired by the United States for $15 million.

At this point Aaron Burr's schemes of conquest were evident when he purchased land from Baron de Bastrop near Natchitoches, Louisiana. Burr proposed a colony that could mount an invasion into Mexico that would provoke the United States into going to war against Spain. This evidently aroused enough fear in Spanish camps in 1806 that troops (1,000 to 1,500) gathered near the Sabine River where they were confronted by Gen. James Wilkinson, commander of United States troops on the southwestern frontier, who ordered his troops back to New Orleans. This eased the tension and also provided the general a chance to distance himself from Burr. The often disputed neutral territory along the Sabine River between the two countries was the result.[3]

Starting with the Gutierrez-McGee Expedition (later called the Republican Army of the North), which entered Texas on August 8, 1812, a period of conflicts pitted Anglo filibusters from the United States against Spanish/Mexican authorities. First came Lt. Agustus W. Magee, a West Point graduate and a tough military man who once ordered about twenty-five robbers, captured in the neutral territory, flogged severely in order to make them reveal the hideout of the rest of their band. Bernardo Gutierrez de Lara was a lieutenant in the United States army who resigned his commission and collected a group of loot-seeking adventurers, took undisputed possession of Nacogdoches.

The Gutierrez-McGee force had no trouble taking Goliad, but McGee died of consumption while in Goliad and was replaced by Samuel Kemper. The invading force was successful in taking San Antonio. Ruthless acts ordered by Gutierrez against the defeated Mexican forces in San Antonio caused dissension and disgust among the ranks of the invading army. Spanish Gen. Joaquin de Arrendondo lured the invaders out of San Antonio into an ambush near the Medina River and almost annihilated the entire army.[4]

The next trio of adventurers to enter the Texas scene was Francisco Zavier Mina, a young Spanish soldier; Don Luis Aury, who had served in the French navy and with French privateers and later moved his operation to Galveston Island; and Col. Henry Perry, a conspirator in the Gutierrez-McGee Expedition. Aury, who had commanded twelve to fifteen vessels in the siege of New Granada, joined forces with Don Jose Manuel Herrera, commissioner of the Morelos government to the United States, and landed a force on Galveston Island on September 1, 1816. In April of 1817 Aury, Mina, and Perry set sail with a fleet of seven ships for the mouth of the Santander River north of Tampico. An argument about who was in command of the land expedition caused Aury to abandon the enterprise and return to Texas on the armed schooner *Commodore* with a few followers. Mina gained minor successes in Mexico, but failed to gain popular support from the natives, and surrendered in November of 1817. Perry became disgusted with Aury and set out overland, arriving finally at La Bahia. He attacked the Spanish fort and evidently had the upper hand until Spanish reinforcements arrived. Most of Perry's men were killed and he blew out his own brains. Thus another chapter in privateers came to an end. Individually, and collectively, these men generated many stories about their real actions but failed to realize their dreams.[5] When this trio abandoned Galveston it left the way clear for Jean Laffite, who occupied the island sometime in 1816–1817.

Dr. James Long entered the scene on a wave of indignation in the United States following the signing of the Florida Treaty, which abandoned any claim the United States may have had in Texas. Setting up shop in Nacogdoches, Long proclaimed Texas to be an independent republic. David Long (James's brother), Captain Walker, and Major Cook established trading houses on the Trinity River and on the falls on the Brazos River and put up a fort below Washington-on-the-Brazos. An unexpected Spanish royalist force, under Colonel Perez, wrecked their plans by killing David Long and forcing Dr. Long to rush to New Orleans for supplies and reinforcements. Long's reorganized forces embarked by boat, landing at Mesquite Landing near San Antonio Bay, just below the confluence of the Guadalupe and the San Antonio rivers, and moved quickly to capture La Bahia. Later they were tricked into laying down their arms. Dr. Long was paroled to Mexico City where he was assassinated by a Mexican soldier.[6] Dr. Long's wife, Jane, remained on Galveston Island with her twelve-year-old Negro servant girl. Mrs. Long gave birth to a baby girl attended only by her servant. She eventually made her way into Austin's colony and played an important part in the War for Independence and during the early years of the Texas Republic, making her final home at Richmond.[7]

Even after the Mexican government began allowing *empresarios* to introduce colonists into Texas, Haden Edwards ran afoul of Mexican authorities in 1826 at Nacogdoches. He attempted to introduce 800 families into the area, but the existence of many old Spanish land titles in the area led to trouble and finally doomed his Fredonian Rebellion. Indians backed the rebellion, but it failed. The rebellion underlined the need to address the problem of overlapping land titles.[8]

In the middle of all of the intrigue, Moses Austin arrived in San Antonio de Bexar on December 23, 1820, seeking a grant to bring colonists into Texas from the United States. Governor Antonio Maria Martinez turned down the request and ordered Austin to leave Texas immediately. Before leaving Bexar, Austin met an old friend, Baron de Bastrop, who interceded with Governor Martinez. Austin got the *empresario* contract he sought. He died before his dream came to fruition. His son, Stephen, accepted the challenge and, after the first settlers met with tragedy, two shiploads of colonists arrived at the mouth of the Colorado River in March of 1822.[9] Colonists began to arrive in Texas at a steady pace after Austin showed the way.

Mexico became alarmed with the unrest among the new colonists and reacted with the Guerrero Decree in 1829, which abolished slavery throughout Mexico. The decree was later rescinded in as far as Texas was concerned.[10] Close behind this turmoil came the law of April 6, 1830,[11] which sought to colonize and garrison Texas with Mexican convicts to overcome the Anglo influence.

The era of Texas history was beginning to open. It was also apparent that the independent-minded people who were carving out new homes on the Raw Frontier wanted to remain free and independent. They staked their lives on these inherent desires.

1.

SPANISH LAND GRANTS

"Nothing ever comes to pass without a cause."[1]

Spanish explorers pushed into present-day Texas in the early 1600s with a settlement founded in Nacogdoches about 1716.[2] But it was not until wild cattle[3] worked their way into the region between the Rio Grande and Nueces rivers that ranchers began to petition the Spanish government for grants of land on, or near, the Nueces River. In the summer of 1749 Jose de Escandon sent Capt. Pedro Gonzales Paredes to set up Villa de Vedoya on the Nueces. It never materialized.[4] Finally, in the summer of 1749 settlers actually set out toward the Nueces, but a drought and an attack by the Apaches kept the settlers from reaching their goal. Escandon never attained his dream of establishing a town on the Nueces River; however, in 1760 ranchers, following herds of cattle, as well as seeking range for an excess of cattle on the Rio Grande, arrived in the area of the present-day Corpus Christi.[5] Before long, wild cattle were roaming the Nueces River valley and joining the herds of Mission Espiritu Santo from Goliad.

The Mission Espiritu Santo had its beginnings at La Salle's old fort on Lavaca Bay, but was moved to a site on the Guadalupe River because the low, marshy location was suspected as causing sickness.

1

It was here that the Spanish started their herd of Spanish cattle that eventually roamed virtually unmolested for scores of years between the Guadalupe and San Antonio rivers. Finally, the mission was moved to Goliad, where the Mission Espiritu Santo became the ranch headquarters. Just across the river the fortress of La Bahia was built. It is estimated that the mission's herd of cattle numbered in the tens of thousands.[6]

A substantial block of Spanish land grants were made in present-day Wilson and Karnes counties, largely in an area known as the Rincon between the San Antonio River and Cibolo Creek. It appears that ranches in this area were granted in the early 1750s; however, these early grants appear to be missing from the Spanish archives in the General Land Office in Austin. The earliest instrument on record is a joint grant issued to Andres Hernandez and Luis Menchaca for fifteen leagues and twelve *caballerias* of land.[7]

Evidently, this area appealed to influential ranchers from La Bahia and Bexar, and in the 1760s ranches along the San Antonio River began to be issued to citizens who had the ear of local officials. El Fuerte de Santa Crus del Cibolo was established in 1736[8] to protect this area. It didn't last long, but was reestablished in 1771.[9]

Historian Robert H. Thonhoff places the Spanish ranches in the San Antonio River area in three major phases: First Spanish Occupation (1734-1737), Second Spanish Occupation (1771-1789), and the Proposed Spanish Occupation (1802). Principal ranches established during the Spanish period were as follows:

RANCHO DE SAN BARTOLO, owned by Hernandez, is credited as being the first private ranch in Texas and also the site of El Fuerte del Cibolo. It was on the Old Mexican Road, later called the Cart Road, which was a main road leading from Indianola to the interior.

RANCHO DE PATAGUILLA contained the present site of the city of Floresville.

RANCHO DE SAN FRANCISCO was owned by Luis Antonio Menchaca and was located between the San Antonio River and Marcelina Creek.

RANCHO DE LA MORA was owned by the Mission San Antonio de Valero and was on the San Antonio River.

RANCHO DE LAGUNA de las Animas belonged to the Delgado and Sambrano families and was on the west bank of the San Antonio River north of Rancho de la Mora.

RANCHO DEL PASO DE LAS MUJERES was on the west bank of the San Antonio River about two miles west of Floresville.

RANCHO DE LOS CHAYOPINES belonged to Francisco Flores de Abrego and takes its name from the Chayopines Indians who occupied the land when the Spanish came to the area.

RANCHO DE RAFAEL was granted to Simon and Juan de Arocha and is in present-day Wilson County.

RANCHO DEL PAISTLE was another ranch owned by the church, this one by Mission Concepcion, and was on the west bank of the Cibolo.

RANCHO DE LAS MULAS was part of the Andres Hernandez grant on the west bank of the Cibolo.

RANCHO DE SAN ANTONIO DEL CIBOLO belonged to Maria Robaina Betancourt.

RANCHO DE SAN MIGUEL DE AMOLADERAS was owned first by Miguel Guerra and later by his widow, Dona Josefa Quinones, and was located near present-day Panna Maria.

RANCHO DEL CLETO, also called RANCHO DE LOS CORRALITOS, belonged to Bernabe Carvajal and was located between the forks of Ecleto Creek and Cibolo Creek.

RANCHO DEL SEÑOR SAN JOSE was granted to Carlos Martinez and located on the west bank of the San Antonio River.[10]

Actually, most Spanish land grants along the Nueces River date back to 1805. However, the forerunner of all of these grants seems to have roots in Casa Blanca, a fortified house, or fort, which was supposedly built in the early 1750s by Don Tomas Sanchez, an army captain from Laredo. Its exact origin is dim, but through the years the old ruins have spawned a multitude of legends—some no doubt true, and others probably the products of some spinner of yarns. But behind every yarn is a grain of truth.

Sanchez was ordered to find a better location for the proposed settlement, and after making a survey, he settled for a location about thirty miles inland on the banks of Penitas Creek a little over a mile from the point where the creek runs into the Nueces River.

The building he built was made out of caliche blocks, called *ciares*, which were cut out of nearby caliche hills. The blocks were rectangular, measuring twelve inches by twelve inches by twenty-four inches, and when dry weighed about 100 pounds. The Spaniards cut these blocks by using a crowbar. The Casa was built in the form of a hollow square with a courtyard in the center. The outside walls were eighteen to twenty feet tall and extended about six feet above the roof line. At each corner a parapet, two *ciares* higher, gave protection for lookouts who had a clear field of vision of the surrounding area. Portholes were placed at intervals above the roof and at two levels in the lower walls. It was built like a fort and legends tell how the settlers took refuge behind the walls during times of Indian trouble.

A feature of the Casa was a well that was dug in the courtyard about five feet square with water found at a shallow depth. On the side next to Penitas Creek artisans crafted a tunnel about one hundred yards long that opened in a clump of brush on the bank of the creek. Evidently the Spaniards were taking into account the unfriendly Indians and bandits who infested the area.

The single door to the Casa was massive, cut out of native cypress trees that grew along the creek. The small windows were covered with heavy wooden shutters and were near the ground. The interior was finished with a smooth white plaster made out of caliche. The plaster was discernible in modern times.

Most of the legends center around the brief period that the Montemayors and Jose de la Garza lived at the old ranch. In fact, "Old Moya" an old ranch hand who worked for Miss Ruth Dodson's father in the area, referred to Casa Blanca as "The Garzarena," evidently referring to the Garza period of occupancy.

Patron Montemayor had three sons and a beautiful only daughter. Old Mexican tales refer to the family as *muy rico* (very rich) since they had large herds of sheep, cattle, and literally hundreds of horses. The family were *gachupins*, or high-class native Spaniards. Their years as lords of the sixteen square leagues* of land were short, as powerful Indian confederations swept through northern Mexico and southern Texas with a wave of murders. One legend claims that the Montemayors were murdered by bandits

---

*A league is approximately 4,428 acres.

who in turn were scalped by the Indians. Montemayor is thought to have sold horses and cattle and brought the money home, but it was evidently never found. It was the lure of this hidden treasure that eventually wrecked the old fort, and even today current owners will find where treasure seekers have plied their trade. Today it takes a guide to reach the spot, which is still marked by mounds of caliche.[11]

Mrs. Wallis Wade, whose husband put together a large ranch in the 1920s to 1940s that included the site of Casa Blanca, liked to spin tales about the ghosts of the past. She at one time set herself the task of reading the entire abstract of the Wade ranch and ended up spending days on the project. John Wade established the ranch, and left each of his three children 15,000 acres.[12]

Casa Blanca became a town with a post office in 1860, closed in 1866, and was reestablished on the SAAP Railroad in 1893. It closed finally in 1922.[13]

Toward the end of the eighteenth century, Casa Blanca was occupied by a priest to serve the needs of the *pastores* (shepherds) and *vaqueros* (cowboys) who took care of the flocks and herds belonging to the missions at Refugio and La Bahia. It was also a refuge for travelers and settlers when Indians were on the move in the area.

When missions were secularized and transferred from monastic orders to the control of the regular clergy, and thus the state, Casa Blanca was affected adversely, as were all other similar small missions.[14]

Evidence of occupation of this land by Spanish settlers can be found in old records dated 1805, wherein Don Cayetano Giron, justice of the settlement of Refugio, ordered a surveyor, Don Cayetano Medrano, to lay out grants south of the Nueces River on a "said tract of land, at the Santa Margarita (San Patricio Crossing) ... and in this vicinity were found a considerable number of wild horses, four indifferent pens for catching the same, droves of deer, wolves, and coyotes and snakes. The ponds and rivers abound with great number of alligators which could injure the large and small cattle."[15]

During this period of 1805 to the Texas War for Independence in 1836, at least fifteen major grants were made south of the Nueces River. They are as follows:

*CASA BLANCA, Juan de la Garza Montemayor and four sons, 1805. 1848, William Mann.

BARRACO BLANCO, Vicente Lopez de Herrera & Sons, Gregoria and Farias, 1806. 1852, James Carter.

RINCON DE LOS LAURELS, Juan Perez Reyes, Juan Perez, Reges Rey, Manuel Garcia, 1806. 1852, Charles Stillman.

PUENTECITAS, Andres Hernandez de la Huente, 1807. 1853, Charles Stillman.

SAN ANTONIO DE AGUA DULCE, Benito Lopez deXaen, 1809. 1858, William Mann.

PADRE ISLAND, Juan Jose de Balli, 1829. 1846, (site still in litigation, but supposed to have passed to Americans by a series of deeds of interests or acreages, the first dated 1846).

VILLAREAL, Enrique Villareal, 1831. 1840, Henry L. Kinney.

EL RINCON DE CORPUS, Ramon de Ynojosa, 1831. 1845, John Schatzell.

SAN ANTONIO DEL ALAMO, Policanpio Farias, 1834. 1845, William H. Lee.

SANTA PETRONILLA, Jose A. Cabasas, 1834. 1845, William H. Lee.

AGUA DULCE, Rafael Garcia, 1834. 1859, Richard King.

PALO ALTO, Mateas Garcia, 1834. 1853, Charles Stillman.

EL CHILTIPIN, Blas Mavia Falcon, 1835. 1880, Mifflin Kenedy.

PASO ANCHO DE ARRIBA, Manuel Farias, 1836. 1857, James Grogan and John L. Haynes.

PASO ANCHO DE ABAJO, Luciano Rivas, 1836. 1857, James Grogan and John L. Haynes.[16]

In present-day Live Oak County there were several Spanish grants. The most interesting was the Ramirez Ranch owned by Don Jose Victoriano Ramirez and son Jose Antonio Ramirez. The ranch was located on Ramirena Creek in the William Primm third league of land. The old ranch house, which was still standing when the first white men entered the county in the early 1800s, was called *Ojo de Aguna de Ramirena*. It was abandoned due to a Comanche raid in

---

*The name of grant is followed immediately by the name and date of the first owner(s). The second date is date the land was entered into the Nueces County land records, followed by the owner.

1813 that killed everyone who had not fled. A Ramirez son petitioned a judge at Mier in 1827 to uphold his family's claim to the land since they had been forced off by Indians when old Fort Ramirez was abandoned by Mexican soldiers during the Mexican War for Independence from Spain.

Tom McNeill, a resident of Live Oak County many years ago, lived on the Ramirena Creek just a few miles from the old Ramirez home/stronghold. He told of talking to a Mexican woman who was near a hundred years of age, who recalled the Indian raid that wiped out the Spanish settlers in the area, including the Ramirez family. McNeill also told stories about the rock pens that were the hiding place for thirty-one muleloads of silver described by Daniel Durham on his death bed in 1873. The rock pens were reputed to be where the Laredo to Goliad road crossed the Nueces River.[17]

Dudley Dobie, a nephew of historian J. Frank Dobie and a historian in his own right, believed that there were at least four incomplete Spanish land grants made in what is now Live Oak County on the west side of the Nueces River and Ramirena Creek. Remains of a very substantial house survived into the late 1800s.[18]

2.

START OF
ARMED CONFLICT

First Blood Shed at Gonzales

A fuse spews and sputters until it ignites the charge that causes an explosion. The fuse that touched off the Texas War for Independence, spewed, sputtered, and at times seemed to go out. When it finally did explode and blood was shed in the Battle of Velasco on June 26, 1832,[1] the explosion was heard throughout Texas, the United States, and Mexico. Perhaps it was not heard around the world, but to the scattered colonists in the Raw Frontier it was a call to arms.

Self-government under Mexico, but free from Coahuila, was the main goal in Texas during this period. It is easy to understand the settlers' position since in the state legislature Coahuila had ten delegates and Texas only two. Texans, and a large number of Tejanos, aligned themselves politically with the Federalists and backed General Santa Anna in his battle to return to the Constitution of 1824, which espoused local control. The Centralists, on the other hand, believed that the state should keep a tight reign on all political activity. By the early to mid-1830s General Santa Anna had abandoned his Federalist ideals and was seen as one of the most tyrannical leaders in the Centralist party. Texas had been largely ignored in Mexico City, but after Stephen F. Austin led the way with Anglo colonists, the population increased rapidly, including a substantial number of Tejanos.[2]

First came local community committees of safety and correspondence as early as 1832, whose main objectives were to organize militia for defense against Indians. To a lesser degree these groups shaped local political thinking. These committees were not hostile toward the Mexicans, but they brought the people together in

Sketch of man on horseback being attacked by Indians on Plains.
By S. B. Enderton.

—Photo courtesy Institute of Texan Cultures

various communities to discuss their problems, which at this time
involved protection against Indian depredations. The Turtle Bayou
Resolutions of June 13, 1832, pledged Texan support for constitu-
tional government. This resolution was an attempt to justify the
attacks on Anahuac and Juan Davis Bradburn. They were written
by Capt. Robert M. Williamson and others assembled at Anahuac,
and circulated throughout East Texas. On October 1 the Convention of 1832 met in San Felipe to ask for governmental reforms
from Mexico. The Convention of April 1833 convened, again in
San Felipe, to correct the weakness of the 1832 document. Finally,
the Consultation of 1835 obtained a quorum in November and
named Branch T. Archer as the president. This meeting pitted the
"war party," led by Henry Smith and John Wharton, against the
"peace party," led by Sam Houston and Don Carlos Barrett.
Stephen F. Austin, who was absent, was counted with the latter
group. The work of the Consultation consisted of setting up a
government for Texas as a state under the Mexican government,
but separate from Coahuila. This provisional government wrote a
document known as the Organic Law, which was greatly flawed
with no clearly defined lines of power. Much of the dissent in the
next few months centered around this lack of a clear leader. The
president and the council could not agree, leading to deadlock.[3]

Between 1832 and 1833 the position of most Texans had
changed from conciliatory to skeptical. When Mexican Gen.
Domingo de Ugartechea sent Cpl. Casimiro de Leon and five soldiers to Gonzales on September 27, 1835, asking Andrew Ponton,
the Gonzales *alcalde*, to return to the Mexican command a small
cannon, the settlers balked. The cannon had been given to Gonzales
residents by the Mexicans in 1831 to protect against Indian raids.
The smoldering fires of resentment against the Mexicans began
to pervade the settlers' previously announced positions of full
cooperation with the authorities. After the first convention of San
Felipe the Mexican government notified the *ayuntamientos* (town
councils) of Austin, Goliad, Liberty, Nacogdoches, and Gonzales
that it looked with extreme disfavor upon participation in the convention. James B. Patrick on April 27, 1833, wrote the political
chief Ramon Musquiz of Bexar, stating that the Gonzales *ayuntamiento* was in favor of Texas being separated from Coahuila. This
brought immediate disagreement from Musquiz.

The DeWitt colonists began to see the "writing on the wall," causing their friendly attitude toward the Mexicans to deteriorate rapidly. It became obvious that General Ugartechea's request for the Gonzales cannon "because it was needed for defense of Bexar" was flawed. The colonists knew that the forts at Bexar had eighteen pieces of unmounted cannon in addition to those already mounted. At this juncture conservative Edward Gritten, secretary to Juan N. Almonte when he visited Texas in 1834 on a fact-finding mission, got the municipality of Gonzales on July 7, 1835, to pass a resolution of loyalty to Mexico. On October 1, 1835, Gritten addressed a letter to Ira R. Lewis, prominent lawyer and member of the Consulation and General Council, recognizing the gravity of the Gonzales face-off, but counseled the municipality of Gonzales to wait for orders from the political chief of the Brazos. The Gonzales colonists became convinced that the Mexicans were set to take away their only weapon of defense. With the realization that they were bucking the Mexican army, the people of Gonzales began to prepare for trouble. Those on the west bank of the Guadalupe River moved into Gonzales. Everyone began to get wagons ready for a possible mass exodus. People in the distant areas buried their possessions and abandoned their cabins. Messengers went out all over Texas asking for help. On September 30 a letter went out to "Fellow citizens of San Felipe and La Baca" signed by Capts. Albert Martin, R. M. Coleman, and J. H. Moore reporting that "a detachment of the Mexican forces from Bexar, amounting to about one hundred and fifty men, are encamped opposite us." As a final act of defiance they buried the Gonzales cannon in George W. Davis's peach orchard and, to erase all marks, the land was plowed.[4]

Gonzales Minutemen

After Thomas S. Saul, member of the Committee of Washington, sent out a letter that started: "Three hundred Mexicans will be tonight in Gonzales," things changed fast. The handful of Gonzales Minutemen swelled to about 160 by October 2, 1835, and when Lt. Francisco Castaneda sought to reclaim the cannon by force he ran

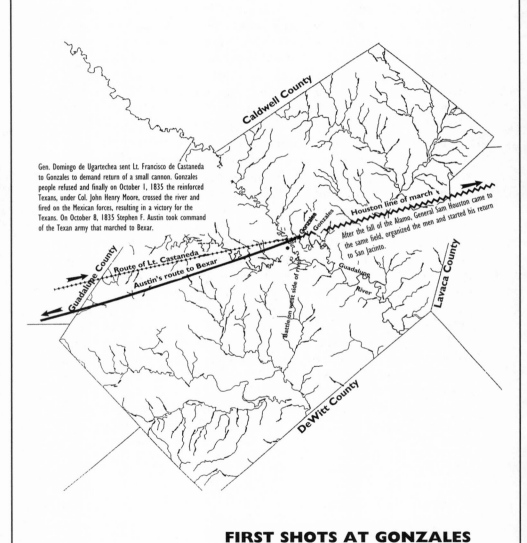

Gen. Domingo de Ugartechea sent Lt. Francisco de Castaneda to Gonzales to demand return of a small cannon. Gonzales people refused and finally on October 1, 1835 the reinforced Texans, under Col. John Henry Moore, crossed the river and fired on the Mexican forces, resulting in a victory for the Texans. On October 8, 1835 Stephen F. Austin took command of the Texan army that marched to Bexar.

Caldwell County

Houston line of march

After the fall of the Alamo, General Sam Houston came to the same field, organized the men and started his return to San Jacinto.

Guadalupe County

Route of Lt. Castaneda

Austin's route to Bexar

Gonzales

Gonzales

Battle on west side of river

Guadalupe River

Lavaca County

DeWitt County

FIRST SHOTS AT GONZALES

into a hail of musketfire from Texans who flaunted a flag that proclaimed: "Come and Take Me." One Mexican was killed and a Texan was wounded.[5] Gonzales became Texas' Lexington as the word spread rapidly all over Texas that a challenge to the Mexican nation had been launched on the banks of the Guadalupe River. Volunteers from different parts of the United States and Texas began moving toward the western frontier. In an attempt to diffuse the situation, Lieutenant Castaneda requested an audience with the Gonzales *alcalde*, Andrew Ponton. Since the *alcalde* was absent, the Mexicans were put off by the frontier settlers/soldiers twice until finally the second *regidor* (Joseph D. Clements) and three other Gonzales men delivered the "no return of cannon" speech. On Thursday night, October 1, the Texans, with their cannon, crossed the Guadalupe River, to the side occupied by the Mexicans, and advanced. Through the fog of early dawn the advance party of Texans drew Mexican fire, with one Gonzales man wounded. The Texans moved their forces forward with the cannon in the center. As dawn broke, so did the battle. Several rounds of cannon fire, followed by accurate musket volleys, forced the Mexicans to retreat and call for a parley. The meeting produced no agreement, and when Lieutenant Castaneda and John Moore retired from the field, the Texans opened accurate fire. The Mexicans fled. The men from Gonzales and volunteers from a wide area had carried the day without the loss of a single man.[6] Despite the victory over the small detachment of Mexican troops, Gonzales was in a perilous position since it was only a few miles to Bexar, where Col. Domingo de Ugartechea was in command of a sizable Mexican force. No doubt this was the catalyst that brought the fragmented colonists together and caused the Mexicans living among the colonists to begin choosing sides.

A circular that was written by Stephen F. Austin in San Felipe on October 3, 1835, and sent all over Texas brought the coming struggle into focus: "What is meant by reforming the Constitution of 1824 . . . In regard to the present movements of the military, the letter from Gonzales, and extracts from other letters of unquestionable faith will inform the public . . . By these letters the people of Texas are informed that their fellow citizens at Gonzales have been attacked—the war has commenced . . . the headquarters of the ARMY OF THE PEOPLE for the present is at Gonzales." On the same day Austin dispatched a letter to James Kerr saying:

"The campaign is opened, and it must not be closed until Bexar is taken and all military is driven from Texas." On October 4 Colonel Ugartechea wrote to Austin expressing hope that the situation could be settled, but stated bluntly that, "I will act militarily and the consequence will be a war declared by the colonists." Austin's position continued to harden and on October 5 he wrote to David G. Burnet that, "I hope to see Texas forever free from Mexican domination of any kind." Any doubt about Austin's thinking vanished.[7]

Troubling News from Mexico

News from Mexico that filtered into Texas during the summer of 1835 was filled with stories of the military activities of Gen. Martin Perfecto de Cos, brother-in-law of General Santa Anna. Cos marched his army into the Federalist state of Coahuila and suppressed their state congress, then moved on to set up headquarters in Matamoros. This was part of the Centralist strategy to change the form of the government. The Catholic Church, which backed centralism, caused memorials to be forwarded from all over Mexico in support of Cos's program. Texans, on the whole, backed the Constitution of 1824 and Federalism. Cos's spies spread news about the general's impending invasion of Texas. An uneasy air of apprehension existed throughout the Raw Frontier. In early October 1835, the *Houston Telegraph and Register* reported that "upwards of a thousand men from San Luis Potosi, and five or six hundred men from Saltillo are now on their march to Texas. These are symptoms of an approaching storm, which is about to discharge itself upon Texas." Evidently the editors had not received word that Cos's army had arrived at Port Copano on September 20, 1835. Patriots on both sides cautioned the other to beware. Thomas Jefferson Chambers, *asesor general* (state attorney) of Coahuila and Texas judge and possessor of multiple land grants, wrote to Texas patriot John J. Linn in Victoria: "I am informed that you are in a great state of alarm, fearful that the general government meditates an attack upon the colonies . . . I am of opinion that your fears are groundless . . ." Linn's militant actions showed that he was not impressed with the letter. He depended upon his own sources in Mexico, where he was a respected trader, who reported that General Santa Anna wanted to be a dictator under the guise of centralism.[8]

General Cos Lands at Port Copano

General Cos arrived at Port Copano aboard the warship *Veracruzana,* accompanied by two other naval vessels, with 500 soldiers and supplies, plus $50,000 in specie to pay for his promised incursion into Texas. Moving inland to Refugio, the general summoned the leaders from the San Patricio, Refugio, and DeLeon colonies and the city of Goliad to gather to pay their respects. He also ordered Capt. Don Enrique Villareal and his officers from Fort Lipantitlan to appear. Before leaving Refugio on October 1, Cos reinforced Fort Lipantitlan and levied requests for money and supplies from San Patricio, Victoria, and Goliad. Officials in Refugio avoided the levy since they furnished most of the carts to move the army's supplies from Copano to Goliad. Cos stayed in Goliad long enough to reorganize his forces, and on October 5 he left for San Antonio, leaving behind a garrison of twenty-seven to guard Fort La Bahia. One of the edicts issued by General Cos reinforced an earlier order for the apprehension and delivery of several Texan and Tejano patriots, including: Lorenzo de Zavala, J.M.J. Carbajal, Juan Zambrano, Moseley Baker, Francis W. Johnson, John H. Moore, William Barret Travis, Samuel M. Williams, and R. M. Williamson. These patriots were to be sent to the interior of Mexico for "trial and chastisement." Historian John Henry Brown marked this order as the beginning of the Federalist War in Texas. Needless to say, these men did not surrender.[9]

Collinsworth Takes Goliad

Shortly after Cos arrived at Copano, Col. James Power, *empresario* of the Refugio Colony, managed to send messengers to nearby settlements warning them of Cos's arrival. Stephen Austin received the warning and immediately dispatched letters calling for "volunteers to rendezvous at League's old place on the Colorado . . . or join it at James Kerr's on La Baca." When the message reached Matagorda, George Collinsworth took charge of raising a force to challenge Cos, gathering at the plantation of Capt. Sylvanus Hatch on October 5.

John J. Linn went to Gonzales in order to get men to "proceed with him" and cut off General Cos on the road from Goliad to Bexar. The plan was to capture Cos and seize the specie that he was carrying. By October 9 Collinsworth's men had been joined by settlers from surrounding areas and were positioned near La Bahia when Ben Milam joined the force. Milam heard the approaching men and hid in the brush, fearing that they were Mexican soldiers. Hearing English being spoken, he called out: "Who are you?"

"American volunteers bound for Goliad, who are you?"

"I am Ben Milam, escaped from prison in Monterey, trying to reach my countrymen in Texas," cried Milam. Milam distinguished himself in Goliad and went on to inspire and lead the forces that stormed and took Bexar from General Cos. Milam died in that assault.

There are several versions of how the old fort of La Bahia was taken. Ira Ingram, company adjunct, wrote in his journal that a group composed of the *alcalde* Juan Antonio Padilla of Victoria, Philip Dimmitt, Dr. Erwin of Refugio, and Colonel Milam sought the surrender of the fort from Lt. Col. Francisco Sandoval. When this failed the volunteers stormed the presidio, broke down the door, and overwhelmed the three officers, twenty-four soldiers, and one cadet. Three Mexicans were killed and one Texan was wounded. The brief battle for the old fortress was over by 11 P.M.[10]

The *Houston Telegraph and Register* on October 28, 1835, reported that Collinsworth's men "marched into the fort by breaking down the door of the church . . . and after a short skirmish . . . the garrison surrendered. There were in the vicinity a considerable number of horses belonging to the military, which, at the time the express (mail) left, had not been taken possession of. Stephen Miller was elected captain. We hope this arrangement will secure our horse, poultry yards &c from the midnight depredations of prowling intruders." Details that seem unimportant now were vital to the participants in 1835.

Very little has been written about the Tejanos from Goliad and Victoria who fought with and assisted Collinsworth in the storming and holding of La Bahia. Some of the Mexicans were captured later and volunteered to join the Federalist cause. Again this list seems to have been lost, or the men later faded into the landscape. As a general rule the Tejanos supported Federalism and thus supported Texas' struggle against the repressive Centralist stance assumed by General Santa Anna.

The victorious Texans sent Captain Sabriego and the other officers (Colonel Sandoval and Cadet Antonio de la Garza). Ensign Juan de la Garza, who was wounded, was given his freedom in Goliad. The other three went to San Felipe where Gen. Stephen F. Austin received them courteously. Sabriego was allowed to return to Goliad where his wife resided. The men were given their freedom in Goliad. It appeared that Cos had stripped the fort of most supplies; however, the Texans found 175 barrels of flour, sugar, coffee, whiskey, and rum, plus an assortment of muskets. Dimmitt immediately ordered a locksmith to repair the guns.[11]

By October 11 the Texan forces at La Bahia had swelled to 180. Capt. Ben Fort Smith was elected to head the new battalion with Collinsworth as the major and Philip Dimmitt the captain. Stephen F. Austin, recently appointed commander-in-chief of the Texas army, ordered that 100 men be retained at Goliad and the remainder dispatched to Bexar.[12] Since most of the men were "chomping at the bit" to fight, most elected to go to Bexar, leaving behind Irish colonists from Refugio and San Patricio, and part of Collinsworth's Matagorda planters. Most of these men had families in the area and wanted to be nearby in order to help move them to safety.[13]

Captain Philip Dimmitt's Commandancy

When Col. Ben Fort Smith and John Alley pulled out of Goliad on October 12 or 13 with the bulk of the troops, headed for Bexar, Capt. Philip Dimmitt was elected commander of the force left behind. This followed the cherished tradition of frontier soldiers that allowed the men to elect their own commander by popular vote. Dimmitt was an ideal man for the job. Born in Kentucky, he came to Texas in 1823 with a letter of introduction to Stephen F.

Austin. He was blunt, brave, and a born leader. He became a trader and married Maria Luisa Lazo, a member of a prominent Tejano family, which gave him standing with the Mexicans. He spoke Spanish fluently. He was soon operating trading posts at Dimmitt's Point, Cox's Landing, Victoria, Bexar, and Goliad. He fully supported Austin's belief that Goliad and La Bahia were keys in Texas' military plans. While not a military man, he had fought Indians with Captain Villareal on the Nueces River and had evidently undergone several brushes with bandits as he protected his trade caravans in and out of Mexico. His name was soon to be known throughout Texas, Mexico, and the United States.[14]

Captain Dimmitt set about immediately to carry out General Austin's order: "You will understand that La Bahia is to be retained."[15] Goliad had been a focal point of military planning as far back as the Spanish period when Bexar, Goliad, and Fort Morgan, on Galveston Island, were considered paramount to any defense of the frontier. Since Dimmitt was familiar with all three outposts, he seems to have been a fitting commander for strategic Goliad in Austin's eyes. He is also credited with bringing military order to the presidio. Most of the men who volunteered at Goliad wanted to do their fighting and go home. They were not accustomed to discipline and felt that if they needed to go home and take care of chores it was their business. With Austin's backing, Dimmitt changed this and is also credited with making substantial repairs to the fort and its walls.

Perhaps Dimmitt's determination to bring discipline to his frontier soldiers had an adverse affect on the Mexican population in Goliad. Dimmitt, with his background, had a thorough understanding of Mexicans living in Texas. This was not true with a lot of his men who had a mistrust for all Mexicans. A goodly number of these Mexicans were staunch Federalists, but there was also an equal number who were die-hard Centralists. As Dimmitt sought to control the situation militarily, rather than work closely with the local *ayuntamientos* and *alcaldes*, the Mexicans began to pull away from supporting Dimmitt wholeheartedly. Actually, there was little control from San Felipe, the seat of government in Texas, over Goliad, Victoria, Refugio, and San Patricio. With the *ayuntamientos* lacking the power or the will to control civil affairs, the military commander in Goliad was the only body to maintain law and order. In this atmosphere the Mexican rancheros became spies and part of Santa Anna's army, causing a great deal of fear and damage in the colonies of DeLeon, Power, and McGloin-McMullen. The Irish colonists in San Patricio petitioned San Felipe, asking permission for their *ayuntamiento* to function according to the old rules.[16]

The Flag of Goliad

Dimmitt is given credit for making the flag of Goliad and Velasco (sometimes called the Brown Flag). On August 27 the commander reported to Austin: "I have a flag made—the colors, and their arrangement the same as the old one—with the words and figures, 'Constitution of 1824,' displayed on the white in the center." Actually, the flag identified with Goliad came to be known as the Bloody Arm flag on a field of blue with red and white stripes.[17]

While Collinsworth was still commander of La Bahia he instigated action that eventually led to the Battle of Lipantitlan. Two Refugio colonists, John Williams and John O'Toole, were commissioned to go to San Patricio to feel out these Irish colonists and seek their support. It was known that the San Patricians were on friendly terms with their Mexican neighbors, as well as the military at La Panticlan, or Lipantitlan.[18] After the two Texan soldiers arrived at San Patricio they were turned over to the Mexican military at La Panticlan, evidently by the colony leaders, and eventually sent to Mexico where it is thought O'Toole died in prison. Williams escaped and returned home and fought with Col. James W. Fannin in the Battle of Coleto, escaping the massacre at Goliad.[19]

Lipantitlan Planned as Check on Texans

Lipantitlan was constructed by Mexico upon the recommendation of Gen. Manuel Mier y Teran. After a fact-finding expedition throughout Texas, he helped pass the law of April 6, 1830, which, among other things, prohibited further immigration into Texas. It was designed to subjugate the people of Texas to the will of Mexico. One part of the law called for building of a new fort on the Nueces River, called Lipantitlan. This new fort, along with La Bahia, Victoria, and Aranzazu on Live Oak Point, all in South Texas, were to be garrisoned with convict-soldiers. It was described by early visitors as "more like a pig pen than a fort." Earthen embankments had been thrown up about five feet high with several log buildings, or *jacales*. (A *jacale* was a crude home made of logs placed upright in a ditch dug the shape of the proposed building. A mortar of mud and manure provided the material to fill the cracks. A thatch roof was held in place by logs resting on the walls.) A deep ditch on the outside of the walls probably furnished the dirt for the walls. A palisade of big logs sunk deep into the ground connected parapets on the corners where cannon could be placed. The location is believed to have been a favorite camping ground for the Lipan Indians. The site is now an ill-kept state park and all that remains of the embankments is a slightly irregular ground surface. Archeological digs performed in the 1980s uncovered a number of artifacts from the "followers camp" adjacent to the fort.[20]

Battle of Lipantitlan

With increasing signs that the Mexican army presence at Fort Lipantitlan represented trouble—not only as a menace to the people of San Patricio who supported the Texan cause, but to the stability of the frontier—Capt. Philip Dimmitt made the decision to mount an attack. Dimmitt arranged with leaders in Matagorda, Refugio, and Lavaca to furnish auxiliary reinforcements and then sent Empresario Power on a reconnaissance to San Patricio for accurate information. In his report Power informed Dimmitt that the cannon, owned by San Patricio, had been seized and taken to the fort and that two bodies of troops were on the way to reinforce existing soldiers. On October 20 Dimmitt informed Austin that he had received twenty men from Matagorda and that he had ordered a detachment of thirty-five men under Adjutant Ira Westover "to proceed forthwith to Le Pantician, the garrison on the Nueces, reduce and burn it."[21]

On October 31, 1835, Westover and Lt. B. Noble left Goliad with thirty-seven men. Another fourteen joined at Refugio and others joined as the contingent left Refugio. After crossing the Aransas River at Aldrete Crossing, they turned to the left on the lower road and arrived at a rancho four or five miles below San Patricio and Fort Lipantitlan.[22] Only partial rosters of this group have been discovered, but researchers like Hobart Huson have estimated that about seventy men took part in the engagement.

It was at this point that Westover learned that Capt. Nicolas Rodriquez had been advised by his spies that a move was to be made against Lipantitlan. Rodriquez gathered a force of about eighty men, crossed the river, and headed toward Goliad on the old Matamoros to Goliad Road. This road was well to the north of Westover's route. As soon as he was informed of his error he turned back toward Lipantitlan. By that time Westover had moved his men from the rancho upriver to a point where he found a canoe that he was able to transport his men to the west side of the river.

Westover's men stumbled upon two Irishmen, one being O'Reilly, who offered to go to the fort and tell the Mexicans to surrender and they would be treated with kindness. The garrison promptly accepted and Westover's men took over the fort, including two four-pound cannons.

In the afternoon of the following day the Texans had begun crossing the river when the Mexican army showed up. The Texans immediately formed a line below the riverbank to meet the Mexicans. The engagement was broken off by the Mexicans when the Texans began to cut them down from their protected advantage. The Texans then crossed the rest of their men; however, due to the late hour and impending rain, the two cannons were dumped into the river. The men then marched to San Patricio where they spent the night, returning the Irish whom they had discovered at Lipantitlan. Nine of the Irish were among Rodriquez's force and three were wounded: the judge, *alcalde*, and sheriff. In all twenty-eight Mexicans were killed or wounded, including Lt. Marcellino Garcia who was brought under a flag of truce to San Patricio to be treated. He eventually died. Only one Texan, William Bracken, was wounded. He had just shot down a Mexican when a ball cut away three of his fingers.[23] The Battle of Lipantitlan was not a turning point or a headline maker; however, it did again focus the attention of the United States on Texas, especially the southern front that was to play a key part in the events leading up to the Alamo and San Jacinto. While it was not known at the time, the Lipantitlan expedition probably forestalled a plan being devised by the Mexican commander to reinforce the Nueces fort to such an extent that the base could be used to launch a strike to retake Goliad. The victory also allowed Governor Viesca and his party to make their move to depart Mexico. Since this was the first Texas victory since Collinsworth took Goliad, it provided grist for newspaper articles in the United States favorable to Texas, leading to a new wave of volunteers.[24]

Gen. Sam Houston had these words to say in his report to the governor and General Council in San Felipe: "I feel much pleasure in the Expression of my approbation in favor of the conduct and bravery of the officers & men who have so handsomely acquitted themselves in the affair [reduction of the garrison of Lipantitlan] and so deservedly won the reputation for themselves and Glory for their Country."[25]

Before Westover and Dimmitt had time to savor the elimination of Fort Lipantitlan, the politics of war swept over them. Gov. Augustin Viesca, deposed Federalist governor of Coahuila and Texas, and his following had managed to leave Coahuila and were headed for Texas, where the governor proposed to reestablish his government over Coahuila and Texas and set up a new capital city in Bexar. Viesca's party was accompanied and protected by twenty Coahuila-Texan cavalry under Col. Jose Maria Gonzales. His entourage included Mariano Yrala, his secretary of state; Vicente Aldrete, land commissioner; Dr. James Grant, member of the council and also a large landholder in Coahuila and Texas; Dr. John Cameron, member of the council; plus several servitors and retainers.

Viesca Versus Dimmitt

While Westover and his forces rested at Aldrete's Crossing on the Aransas River, the Viesca party overtook them. Since John Linn and Empresario Power, members of Westover's forces, were well acquainted with Viesca and some of his party, they extended a welcome, inviting them to stop over in Refugio. This gave Westover time to go ahead and break the news that the governor was on his way to Goliad. It was Viesca's wish to be welcomed as the head of state (Coahuila and Texas) when he arrived in Goliad. Dimmitt did not believe it was in his province to enter into the political realm, and while he did welcome Viesca, he did not roll out the "royal carpet," thus injuring the governor's inflated ego. The furor brought a flood of complaints to Stephen F. Austin, especially from the Centralist Mexicans, against Dimmitt. Austin relieved Dimmitt of his post as commander of La Bahia on November 21. The deposed commander packed his bag and was ready to leave when the entire command held a meeting demanding that their leader be reinstated. The resolution was brought forth by a committee composed of J. W. Baylor, B. Noble, John P. Borden, Benjamin J. White, Sr., and Dugald McFarlane. Sixty-seven men signed the resolution. Eventually the General Council quashed the action against Dimmitt, reinstating his command at Goliad.[26]

Goliad's Declaration of Independence

Dimmitt maintained a tight ship at Goliad and continued working to strengthen the fort. When the siege of Bexar appeared to be reaching its final stage he took several of his associates and went to Bexar in time to participate in the final assault on December 5. He returned to his command shortly after General Cos surrendered. After returning to Goliad Dimmitt became obsessed with the idea that it was time for Texas to divorce itself from the Federalist movement and consider the question of independence for Texas. To put this plan in motion he called a meeting for all citizens in the Goliad area to meet at La Bahia on Sunday, December 20, to consider the question of independence. Dimmitt was elected chairman of the meeting and Ira Ingram the secretary. The Goliad Declaration of Independence grew out of the convention and was eventually signed by ninety-six men. The document contained much of Dimmitt's philosophy; however, it was couched in Ingram's eloquent language since as secretary he put the finishing touches on the work.

After the signing ceremony, the Goliad flag, sometimes called the Bloody Arm flag, was raised amid cheers from soldiers and citizens alike. Nicholas Fagan, Refugio colonist, is credited as being the soldier who raised the flag. The declaration and flag-raising can be attributed to the staunch patriotism of Dimmitt, a real Texas patriot. The declaration was sent to the General Council in San Felipe on December 30 and on January 3, 1836, they denounced it. The sting of this denunciation was lessened, however, when General Austin expressed himself as being for independence.[27] No doubt the Centralists in Goliad kept a low profile.

Dimmitt and his men had been the focal point of the southern front for several months without receiving material assistance from the provisional government. His men with families were desperate for a means to support their home folks. The condition of the bankrupt command was brought to a head by the arrogant actions of Dr. Grant, who, together with Frank W. Johnson, planned a bold military stroke at Matamoros, and demanded that Dimmitt give them supplies for their self-serving expedition. Grant and Johnson had been granted permission by the General Council to mount an attack on Matamoros, a movement that Gen. Sam Houston opposed. When Grant's force arrived in Goliad and saw the Dimmitt flag flying over the old mission, Grant threatened to tear it down by force, saying it offended him. Grant had extensive land holdings in Coahuila and was one of those who accompanied Viesca to Goliad, demanding that Dimmitt recognize the deposed governor as the legal head of Coahuila and Texas. Dimmitt took the flag down the next day to avoid bloodshed among Texans and gave the freebooters part of his meager supplies. Grant repaid his generosity by seizing most of the fort's *caballos* (horses) and pressing other property from local citizens.

With the defeat of Cos at Bexar, plus the fact that Dimmitt's command was running low on supplies, most of the men began to "itch" to move to a more active front or return home. On January 10, 1836, Dimmitt held the final muster and prepared to abandon the old fort. Discharges were issued to deserving soldiers and on December 11 and 12 the troops started leaving. Captain P. S. Wyatt, with a group of volunteers from Alabama, was placed in charge of La Bahia. Dimmitt and a core of loyal followers left on December 13 toward Victoria, meeting Gen. Sam Houston and his staff the following day. Houston had arrived at Port Copano to attempt to dissuade volunteers from joining the Matamoros expedition planned by Grant, Johnson, and Fannin.[28]

Houston believed that the old port of Copano was the key to military success against the Mexicans. His strategy called for

Copano to be denied as a port for the Mexican army, forcing them to bring supplies overland to support any army camped in Texas. In December of 1835 he advised Gov. Henry Smith: "under any circumstances the port of Copano is important . . . Colonel Wyatt with two attachments of auxiliary volunteers, is on his way to the vicinity of Copano . . . so essential to the present posture of our affairs." He continued to direct men and supplies to the port, arriving in the area himself on December 14.[29]

The focus of the coming storm in Texas would be concentrated for the next few weeks on the city of San Patricio, where Grant and Johnson went to prepare for their invasion of Matamoros. After General Houston and others had talked to the incoming troops, as well as those following Grant and Johnson, slightly less than one hundred men chose to follow the dream of choking off the Mexican army by striking at Matamoros. When Houston learned the broad authority of the orders given to Grant, Johnson, and Fannin, he felt powerless to direct Texas troops. As a result he returned to San Felipe and secured a furlough and went on a mission with Indians who were menacing the colonial borders. He was hopeful that when the convention met in March his authority would be increased. Historian Brown placed the number following Johnson and Grant at sixty-four, so perhaps Houston's speeches were not wasted.[30]

3.

TEXAS POLITICAL REALITIES IN 1835~36

A brief look at the government of Texas during this troubled period is necessary in order to understand the actions taken by Sam Houston, Stephen F. Austin, Frank W. Johnson, James Grant, James Fannin, and Philip Dimmitt. Through a series of meetings, representatives from a majority of Texas communities formed a government on November 7, 1835, at San Felipe. The new government put power in the hands of a General Council, which received its power from an instrument known as the Organic Law.

It should be noted that this was the third deliberative body assembled in Texas, the first being formed on October 1, 1832, and the second on April 1, 1833—both in times of peace. The November 1835 meeting, however, was held with battles underway—first at Gonzales, then at Goliad, and then at Concepcion. The Battle of Lipantitlan took place on November 3-4. In fact, the hostilities caused several of the representatives from the Raw Frontier to miss part of the meeting at which Henry Smith was elected governor and James W. Robinson was made lieutenant governor. Lines of power were never clear between the governor and the council.

In January of 1836 relations between the governor and the council reached an impasse when Governor Smith demanded that the General Council resign: "your services are now no longer needed, until the convention meets." Later the same day the council countered by impeaching Smith: "Resolved, that Henry Smith,

Governor of the Provisional government of Texas, be ordered forthwith to cease the functions of his office, and be held to answer to the General Council." Later the council installed Robinson as acting governor.

Earlier, Sam Houston had been named major general of the Texas army by the General Council on November 12, 1835. The General Council, at Col. James Fannin's urging, established an auxiliary volunteer corps. Houston then appointed Fannin a colonel in the regular army and on December 10 the council ordered Fannin to enlist reinforcements and act as an agent of the provisional government.

Frank Johnson was appointed adjutant and inspector general under Gen. Stephen F. Austin, also by the council, and issued a call for a Federal army to fight under the Mexican flag of 1824. Dr. James Grant had like authority, which caused him to enter into a tenuous agreement with Johnson for a Matamoros expedition. Stephen F. Austin was removed from the mix when he was sent by the council to the United States to raise money for the struggling colony.

Add to this mixture the fact that troops reserved the right to elect their own commanders and you have a jungle of mixed commands presided over by officers with inflated egos.[1]

The General Council at times sought to micro-manage government, especially in the appointment of military leaders. Almost any member of the council could get a favorite named to any post in the military, regardless of his experience. This made for more than one man being named to conduct a project and not have to answer to the commander-in-chief. If this was not enough of a mix the Federalists and Centralists each had an agenda they sought to put into effect. The council did not trust the president, a feeling that was mutual. Frontier conditions made it impossible for delegates to attend all meetings, leaving important matters to be decided by a few nearby delegates. Few of the delegates remained in office for the entire "war period."[2]

Mexicans Remain Loyal to Their Native Land

There were a large number of Mexicans who remained loyal to Mexico, but continued to live on their ranches and in the towns among the Anglo colonists. Some of these became effective spies for the Mexican forces. Others worked hard to stay out of trouble with either side. Some Mexicans chose to fight with the Texans.

One of the first instances of how impressive this espionage network could be was seen when Gen. Jose Urrea was gathering his army at Matamoros while the Texans were organizing and gathering troops at Copano and Refugio in the fall of 1835. These spies kept the Mexican general aware of the movement of the Texan forces on an almost daily basis. This information allowed the Mexicans to capture a detachment of Tennessee volunteers under Maj. William P. Miller when they arrived at Port Copano on March 21, 1836.[3] Later, when Col. James Fannin was attempting to extract colonists from Refugio, General Urrea's advance knowledge of the Texan's plans allowed him to send Capt. Pretalia and thirty civilians, headed by Goliad ranchero Don Guadalupe de los Santos, to conduct a holding operation. Meanwhile, the general, with 100 horsemen and 180 infantry, moved into place to keep Lt. Col. Ward's forces pinned at the mission in Refugio.[4] The rancheros also captured a messenger whom Col. James Fannin sent to Ward in Refugio to tell him that he was abandoning Goliad on Houston's orders. This action enabled Urrea to get some of his advance troops in place to slow the movement of Fannin's men until his main force arrived.[5] Another ranchero supplying information was Don Carlos de la Garza, of the Carlos Ranch. A number of Karankawa Indians fought with the rancheros.[6]

Alert Mexican colonists also furnished information to Urrea in such detail that he knew of the movements of Col. Frank Johnson and Col. James Grant so accurately that both forces were slaughtered at the Battle of San Patricio and the ambush at Banquete.[7]

A lot of the success that General Urrea enjoyed in his sweep to destroy Colonel Fannin at Goliad came from loyal Mexicans in and around Lipantitlan, San Patricio, Refugio, and Goliad. All of the names of the loyal Mexicans have never been discovered; however, some of the more famous, or notorious, depending upon your point of view, have been documented.[8]

One loyal Mexican who received recognition in tracking down stragglers from the battles in Refugio was Capt. Juan Moya, a rancher who lived on one-quarter league of land he had received on December 3, 1834. This ranch was on the Blanco Creek about halfway between (present-day) Berclair and Refugio. At one time the wily captain gathered over one hundred horses at his ranch, which he planned to turn over to the Mexican army along with a regular flow of supplies. Capt. Philip Dimmitt, commander at Goliad, learned about the plan and sent James Kerr and Ira Westover with twenty men to seize the horses. Forewarned by informants in Goliad, Moya was one step ahead of the troops and escaped with his horses to Lipantitlan. Earlier, when Gen. Martin Perfecto de Cos arrived at Port Copano in September of 1835, Moya was one of the first to offer his services.[9]

Moya remained active during hostilities. Evidently, since the Moya ranch was isolated, the Moya family managed to return to their land some time after the revolution to live quietly. During the period immediately following the Civil War, and during the Cart War when conditions in Goliad County were perilous to all Mexicans, the Moyas were accused of being involved in a crime. The result was that the home of the Moyas, which legends describe as being a "fortress," was attacked by a group of Goliad Minute Men. Sometime during the attack Goliad County Sheriff Phil Fulcrod promised safety to Juan and his two sons, Marcelo and Antonio, to go to Goliad to answer the charges. En route a group of Minute Men, led by Capt. Coon Durham, waylaid the sheriff and his prisoners and shot the Moyas, without interference from the sheriff or any of his dozen deputies. Other accounts say the Moya men were hanged.

A portion of this land is still owned by the Moya family. In March of 1975 the Moya descendants sought to reclaim the land in their original grant through a suit filed in Bee County. After a trial, Judge Ronald Yeager of the Thirty-sixth District Court ruled in favor of the heirs of John J. O'Brien, current owners of most of the disputed Moya Mexican grant.[10]

Goliad was something of a center for Mexican resistance to the Texan cause. The Mexican residents professed support for Fannin, but evidently were fearful of being too cooperative. The probable leader was Capt. Carlos de la Garza who had a ranch home on the San Antonio River. The Mexican sympathizers in Goliad gravitated to the captain's ranch where riders were dispatched on a regular basis destined for Mexican forces.[11]

When Agustin Viesca, deposed governor of Texas and

Coahuila, escaped from his enemies in Monclova, Mexico, and together with a guard and trusted friends, entered Texas, he came first to Goliad. It was Viesca's intention to set up an interim government in Bexar. As mentioned earlier, Capt. Philip Dimmitt was in command at Goliad on November 11, 1835, when the deposed governor arrived, expecting to be greeted as a visiting head of state. Dimmitt did not believe he had the authority to accord Viesca with such recognition; however, he did send an advance party to greet the governor and escort him into Goliad.[12] The Mexicans who were loyal to Mexico in the Goliad area took this opportunity to try and embarrass Dimmitt by charging that he had mistreated the Mexican population in Goliad. Goliad's *alcalde*, Roberto Galvan, openly criticized Dimmitt. On March 9 or 10 Goliad's *alcalde* at that time, Encarnacion Vasquez, was captured by Captain King's men while on a relief mission to remove Refugio ranchers from an assault by General Urrea's forces. Vasquez was riding with a group of rancheros plundering homes of the Refugio settlers.[13]

While Goliad seemed to be the center of Mexican opposition to any political arrangement that separated Texas from Mexico, Bexar Tejanos were in the forefront in fighting alongside the Texans, especially in the early days of the revolution. When General Cos moved his army into Bexar in October of 1835 he experienced problems with the native Mexican population. Gen. Stephen F. Austin indicated that his forces were fed information by deserters from the Mexican army on an almost daily basis. One case involved Macedonia Arocha, a member of Cos's army, who went back and forth at night to Juan Seguin's company in the Texan army and to visit his family who lived in Bexar. In this manner the Texan forces were provided an almost daily report of the morale of Cos's force. At one time Austin advised two of his company commanders, Col. James Bowie and Col. James Fannin, of "two companies of the army of Cos to desert and come out at a given signal." It will be discussed later that a deserter from Cos's army provided information that caused the Texans, under Col. Ben Milam and Col. Frank Johnson, to successfully launch an attack that defeated Cos.[14]

General Cos alienated the Bexar Mexicans even more by forcing old dons to do menial tasks. Erasmo Seguin, and others of like stature, were forced to sweep the public square and make their women grind corn for the soldiers. A number of prominent

Mexicans found it expedient to leave town and live with nearby friends or hide out in town. Cos also removed Seguin from his office in the *ayuntamiento*.[15] Austin sought to capitalize on the Mexicans' disenchantment by issuing a proclamation that said, in part, "no citizen will be persecuted nor molested in any way in either their persons or property on account of their political opinions." Houston urged anyone wishing to embrace the plan to present themselves to the army of Texas.[16] Today such a proclamation would probably be labeled as "purely political." In 1835 it caused the Mexicans to view anyone going back and forth between the two sides as Texas spies rather than informants to their native land. Few profited, and many became suspicious of their neighbors. As the food needs of both armies put an increasing strain on the local economy, conditions became strained between all parties. Since the Texas army did not have funds with which to purchase foodstuffs, they were forced to impress supplies when farmers or merchants would not cooperate. The Texans who controlled most of the rural area became suspicious of Mexican farmers who refused them corn, accusing them of holding it for the Mexicans who could afford to pay. It was a no win situation.[17]

Irish Who Aided the Mexican Cause

Without a doubt a number of Irish settlers in the San Patricio colony of James McGloin and John McMullen gave aid to the Mexican cause. Historians question why this colony helped the Mexicans while the Irish settlers in the James Power and James Hewetson Colony were stalwarts behind the Texas struggle for independence. The background on the men behind each colony seems to be the key to the answer.

James McGloin and John McMullen met either in Ireland or in Matamoros. They were related by marriage—McGloin married McMullen's stepdaughter, Eliza (Espades) Cummings, either in Savannah, Georgia, or Matamoros in 1825.[18] The early history of both men is unclear, but they were business partners in a mercantile enterprise in Matamoros. It is believed that Eliza Cummings was of Spanish descent, which perhaps helped cut through Mexican red tape and led to the granting of an *empresario* contract to McMullen and McGloin. McMullen spoke Spanish fluently and probably was the lead man in negotiations with officials in securing the *empresario* grant. Both men had many friends in Matamoros, as well in other centers of Mexican affairs.

Irish immigrants from New York settled in the San Patricio de Hibernia Colony on the Nueces River. It appears that communications were maintained with McGloin's and McMullen's friends in Matamoros, and to cement these relations, starting in 1832 a yearly feast was held on the banks of Banquete Creek with Mexican families from Matamoros joining the Irish from San Patricio. Susanna O'Docharty is credited with promoting this holiday feast. The new Irish settlers depended heavily on the Mexican ranchers in the area for advice on how to survive and establish cattle ranches on their newly acquired land. These Irish settlers came from an area in Ireland where a couple of acres was a large estate, so naturally learning to make a living by ranching an area as large as a county in Ireland was completely foreign. Help from the Mexicans was sought and appreciated and was probably the difference in surviving in a hostile environment.[19]

The two groups had still another bond since both were Roman Catholic. With these strong ties it is small wonder that some San Patricio settlers were recorded as fighting with the Mexicans when hostilities broke out in 1835. On October 17, 1835, Capt. Philip Dimmitt, commander of Goliad forces, outlined the problem in a dispatch to Gen. Stephen Austin: "It is rumored that the people of St. Patricio have joined the military at the Nueces." After penning this statement Dimmitt added a note that put the situation into focus: ". . . that two of our men, dispatched with letters from Linn and others in San Patricio, five days ago, are prisoners, and in irons, in Le Panticlan."[20]

It was obvious that other leaders in the area were worried about the people in San Patricio. On October 8, 1835, Thomas Western, a patriot and merchant in Goliad, wrote to John McMullen and James McGloin, admonishing them: "the hour has arrived when it has become necessary to call upon you for your co-operation in promoting the cause of liberty and the Constitution of 1824 . . . this place is ours decidedly and more immediately wish your aid . . ." Earlier, John J. Linn had written to Thomas Henry, *alcalde* of San

Patricio, urging his cooperation with the Texans gathered in Goliad at La Bahia.[21]

At least nine of the Irish of San Patricio took part in the Battle of Lipantitlan, fighting with the Mexican forces, and three were wounded, namely the judge, *alcalde*, and sheriff. After the battle the Texan soldiers sought shelter in San Patricio, where they were well received. The next day a flag of truce was sent in from the Mexican force asking "permission to send in a Mexican wounded to receive surgical attention, they having no surgeon." The wounded arrived a few hours later, and among them was the second officer in command, Lt. Marcellino Garcia, who was mortally wounded and died the next day.[22]

John Williams and John Toole, members of Dimmitt's force and Refugio colonists, were the volunteers who went to San Patricio to ascertain the true relations between the Irish and the Mexicans at Fort Lipantitlan. Both were taken prisoner and sent to Mexico. Toole escaped and returned to fight against the Mexicans. Williams is thought to have died in a Mexican prison.[23]

John J. Linn wrote to Austin concerning San Patricio: "It is reported that the people of San Patricio have joined the soldiers but generally supposed that it was through necessity, they must of course be on the right side or they will belie their countryman . . ."[24]

The exact number of Irish families who moved to Mexico during this period is hard to determine since no one wanted to lose title to their land in San Patricio Colony. It should be noted that a law had been passed by the legislature that anyone who fought against Texas would forfeit their land. In most cases the families moved to Matamoros without fanfare, and then sometime after the hostilities were over they returned to Texas and took up their lives where they left off. Naturally, few who chose to leave the country or move to another part of the state talked openly about where they were when the fighting of the Texas Revolution took place.

However, several families made no secret of their Mexican leanings. Probably the most prominent family was that of Susanna and William O'Docharty. In December of 1835 John Turner, Texas patriot and San Patricio colonist, intercepted two letters between Mexican authorities at Lipantitlan and the O'Dochartys. In his letter to Governor Smith, Turner said: "The husband of this woman is known to be the leader of the Partozans (partisans of Centralism) in this town and his wife is said to lead him and legislate for all."[25] Shortly after the Battle of San Jacinto the O'Dochartys set an example that other colonists followed by going to Matamoros. Several members of the Hart families were among the first wave moving to Mexico. Bridget Hart, whose husband Felix was assassinated near San Patricio in 1834, went to Mexico with her three children, Catherine, Timothy, and Ann. The widow and her three children made the trip unaccompanied in an oxcart across the rough land between the Nueces and Rio Grande rivers. Catherine married David Craven in Matamoros and later they went to Louisiana. Bridget married a man by the name of Smith. All eventually returned to their land near Papalote without fanfare after the end of the war. Members of the Hart family are buried in the Papalote Cemetery.[26] After arriving in Matamoros Susanna O'Docharty ran an ad in the local newspaper seeking students for a school she had started. After the war, probably in the late 1840s when partial law and order had returned to San Patricio, the O'Docharty family moved back and took their place as leaders in the old colony. Susanna, undoubtedly a woman of iron will, was troubled about a baby who died at birth and was buried in Matamoros, and so she and twelve-year-old Hubert Timon made the perilous trip by horseback to Matamoros and returned with the baby's casket on the horn of her saddle. It was buried in the Old Cemetery on the Hill in San Patricio.[27]

It is believed that in addition to the families who went to Matamoros from San Patricio a number of other colonists went to either Victoria or Houston. Census records of 1850 indicate some were still living in these cities since the old town of San Patricio was considered a "depopulated" community. The same citizens were not listed in later census rolls. More information about the people who fled from San Patricio Colony will be found in volume two of the *Raw Frontier*.

McGloin was also on record as questioning support of the Constitution of 1824. When he received an appointment as judge of the San Patricio municipality from Lewis Ayers, commissioner of the governor's office, in December of 1835, he declined with these words: "I decline taking the oath until I hear an explanation of the last paragraph of the oath which seems to me not to accord with the spirit of the federal constitution . . ."[28]

The oath that he objected to read: "I do solemnly swear that I will support the republican principles of the Constitution of 1824, and obey the Declaration and ordinances of the Consultation of the chosen delegates of all Texas in General Convention assembled and the ordinances and decrees of the Provisional Government; and I will faithful perform and execute the duties of my office agreeable to law, and to the best of my abilities so help me God."

Without a doubt the Irish Catholic settlers of the old colony of San Patricio had strong convictions and would not compromise them in any way.

4.

VOLUNTEERS GATHER
AT GONZALES

It will be remembered that the Gonzales Minute Men success-fully routed the Mexican forces under Lieutenant Castaneda on October 2, 1835; however, it did not erase the Mexican menace. Col. Domingo de Ugartechea still had a sizable force in Bexar. The *Houston Telegraph and Register* on October 10, 1835, emphasized the gravity of the situation: "Colonel Ugartechea is on his march from Bexar with 500 men, to overrun our country. They come to make us yield to unconditional and slavish submission to a military usurpation. They came to fasten down upon our necks the yoke, and to rivet upon our hands the manacles of a military servitude. Gonzales is doomed to the sword and the flame." Gen. Perfecto Cos, with additional troops, was on the march from Goliad to Bexar, leaving Goliad on October 5, 1835, and probably arriving in Bexar about a week later.

Stephen F. Austin Assumes Command

Cos and his reinforcements presented a real threat to Texas. To meet this challenge, volunteers from all parts of Texas continued to pour into Gonzales. The Texans decided that Bexar must be attacked as soon as possible. A leader was needed. Early on the morning of October 11 the self-annointed leaders from the various freedom-seeking groups met to name a commander-in-chief. It soon became obvious that each group wanted a big voice in the election. Those with smaller numbers threatened to leave if their leaders were not considered. Fortunately for the affairs of Texas, Stephen F. Austin rode into camp about 1 P.M. on October 11, 1835, to turn the bickering into a unified vote of confidence for the "Father of Texas." He took over immediately. On the 13th of October they formed a regiment with John Moore as colonel, Edward Burleson as lieutenant colonel, and Alexander Sommervell as major. Austin named the staff consisting of Warren D. C. Hall, adjutant and inspector general; David B. Macomb, assistant; Peter W. Grayson and William T. Austin, aides-de-camp; William H. Jack, brigade inspector; and William H. Wharton, judge advocate.[1]

Austin had set the tone for the reaction to the Mexican threat when he issued a circular to the people of Texas on October 3, 1835. It closed with these ringing words: "... fellow citizens at Gonzales have been attacked ... the headquarters of the ARMY OF THE PEOPLE for the present is at Gonzales ... This committee exhorts every citizen who is yet at home, to march as soon as possible ... Texans must be freed from military despots before it is closed."[2]

It should be noted that Austin did not accept the command of the troops willingly. His health had been deteriorating since his return from a twenty-eight month absence from San Felipe, most of the time spent in a jail in Mexico City. He returned to Texas in August of 1835 and reluctantly agreed to accept the command. All groups recognized Austin as a true patriot who put his allegiance to his adopted state above his own personal well-being.

Organization of the army under Austin proceeded rapidly and on the 12th of October the troops started crossing the Guadalupe River and by the 13th they were on the march for Bexar.[3]

On October 26 from Camp Salado (near Bexar) Austin sent the following dispatch to the Permanent Council: "I shall move with the Army today to the Missions, and press the operation as fast as my force will permit—I have but four hundred effective men—General Cos has about 800 or 900—there has been skirmishing daily but no loss on our side."[4]

William H. Jack, a Texas militant who was active at Anahuac, as well as the assumed author of the Turtle Bay Resolutions, wrote to Austin from Goliad on October 13, advising him: "I give it as my decided opinion, that an engagement ought not to be risked, unless success is next to certain." R. R. Royall was more encouraging, saying that "70 muskets, seven pieces field Cannon, powder, Lead etc. Four wagons will leave [San Felipe] tomorrow." John Wharton advised that one or two wagons would leave Columbia on October 14. Other offers of supplies and men came to Austin from San Felipe and Goliad. Benjamin Fort Smith brought to Austin's attention the fact that frontier soldiers were not apt to stay inactive in camp for a lengthy period of time before deserting. Philip Dimmitt, commander at Goliad, gave Austin some good news to reflect upon that he picked up while talking to a deserter from Cos's army: "All the Bexar troops will join the Americans, as soon as they present themselves; that, the officers and infantry want a fight, but that the cavalry do not...." The following day Dimmitt intercepted another message that indicated that Cos was actively fortifying Bexar.[5] Austin knew from long experience that advice was offered freely, but it was the commander who had to make up his mind and issue the orders.

Battle of Mission Concepcion

On the 27th of October Austin ordered Col. James Bowie and Capt. James W. Fannin, with ninety-two men, to select a suitable campground as near as possible to San Antonio. Camp was made in a crescent-shaped bend of the San Antonio River, two hundred yards distant from Mission Concepcion. A heavy fog the next morning shrouded movement of the enemy, which completely encircled the small detachment of Texans. An advance guard of Mexican cavalry rode into the Texan line and almost ran over the sentinel, Henry W. Karnes. The exchange of fire alerted the frontier soldiers, and due to some excellent marksmanship, the Texans held their own against the mounted Mexicans. The Texans had the advantage of a hill in between them and the enemy and were able to fire and then fall back in safety to reload. The Mexicans brought up a brass double-fortified four-pounder and used it to rake the Texans' hill. Sharpshooters managed to keep the cannon silent most of the time. "The cannon and victory" became the battle cry and the long rifles continued to pick off the artillery men. Four charges by the Mexican cavalry were broken, causing the enemy to sound retreat before the main body of Austin's men reached the scene. Leaders in the battle—Bowie, Karnes, and Fannin—believed that had the main army arrived in time they could have decisively defeated the Mexicans. One Texan (Richard Andrews) was killed while the Mexicans suffered one hundred casualties.[6] The frontier leaders were all for attacking while the Mexicans were in retreat, but the opportunity was lost.

The Texan army now numbered about 800. Austin failed to push his advantage, saying he favored waiting for the arrival of heavy guns before carrying on with the assault. He especially wanted the heavy guns to batter down the walls of the Alamo. R. R. Royall,[7] a patriot from Matagorda, had taken over as president of the council from Austin in San Felipe and made numerous efforts to get men and supplies for the army at Bexar. His efforts were hampered due to those on the council who were critical of the San Antonio Campaign. Ben Milam and James Bowie, as well as other militants on the council, were for forthright action. As a result of the delay, the force that at one time probably reached 900 fighting men diminished to 500. Frontier soldiers wanted immediate action in almost any situation. Camp life was not to their liking and they would just as soon pack up and go home.[8]

Austin was not completely alone in his battle strategy. Early in November he held a council of twenty-six officers on the question of storming San Antonio or trying to starve out the army and citizens. The vote was twenty-five to one against storming the town. There were at least three minor skirmishes during November.

Austin made his move on November 21, 1835, when he announced that the army would storm Bexar the next day. Later the same day, Col. Edward Burleson and Phillip A. Sublett, both captains of companies, informed Austin that the "majority of them are opposed to the measure, and are unwilling to attempt it." Later the same day, after receiving the recommendations, Austin countermanded the orders for storming the town. On November 24 Austin announced that he would be leaving to take the appointment as commissioner to the United States. When the troops were polled to see how many would remain in San Antonio, only 405 agreed, and of these sixty-four were newly arrived New Orleans Grays. The troops elected Col. Edward Burleson to fill Austin's job as the new commander. Others named were Francis W. Johnson as his adjutant general, and Peter W. Grayson and William T. Austin as his aides-de-camp.[9]

Grass Fight

A slight comic diversion eased the tension on November 26 when a Mexican force was seen escorting a pack train loaded with sacks. It had been rumored that a Mexican force was en route to Bexar with a large amount of silver to pay troops and purchase needed supplies. Bowie, who was on patrol with a detachment of one hundred men, mounted an immediate attack on the train, while sending word to camp requesting reinforcements. Confusion reigned as Bowie's cavalry charged in immediately while those on foot followed into the fray. Just about that time Texan reinforcements from camp arrived on the scene. The Mexicans abandoned their pack animals and fled to town. The victors ripped into the sacks, but to their dismay they were loaded with grass destined for the Mexican cavalry horses, and not silver. This came to be known as the "Grass Fight." No doubt Bowie's men were nicknamed the "reapers of silver grass."[10]

The Siege and Fall of Bexar

The deciding moment in whether to storm Bexar or retire to winter camp in Gonzales came after Col. Edward Burleson, following orders of the General Council, started to break camp, leaving General Cos in control of San Antonio. Most of the men had come to fight General Cos's army and they were in no mood to follow orders from the General Council. Troops were gathered around Burleson's tent to vent their feelings when a Mexican army officer, Capt. Jesus Comanche Cuellar, who had deserted from Cos's army, came into camp and sought to talk to the commander. A meeting was arranged, including a group of dissatisfied Texan soldiers. The deserter reported that the Mexican defenses were weak and that the men were disheartened and wanted to quit. At this point Col. Frank W. Johnson threw down the challenge: "Who will go with old Ben Milam into San Antonio?" Ben Milam, a truly great leader, was always in the center of any action.[11]

More than 300 men quickly volunteered and were divided into two divisions. Colonel Milam was named commander of the first division, with Major R. C. Morris of the New Orleans Grays as second in line. Colonel Johnson was put in charge of the second division, aided by Col. W. T. Austin and Col. James Grant. This was on December 4, 1835.

Several days of house-to-house fighting saw the Texans close in on the Mexican army, which had taken refuge in the Alamo. After Milam was killed in action, Johnson was named the chief commander. At 6:30 A.M., December 9, the Mexicans sent out a flag of truce, and on December 14 General Burleson sent a message to Governor Smith reporting that Bexar had been taken. Colonel Johnson was proclaimed a hero, along with Ben Milam. No sooner had the shooting stopped than Johnson, together with Grant and Fannin, began to formulate plans for an armed expedition to Matamoros.

The news of the victory reached San Felipe and the General Council drew up an address directed to Gen. Edward Burleson, Col. F. W. Johnson, and all the brave officers and soldiers of the citizen volunteer army in Bexar. The address was full of praise for the citizen soldiers and ended with a glowing salute: "Your joy is our joy, your sorrows, our sorrows; and with assurance of unabating sympathies with you and all our fellow citizens in the present glorious epoch in our country's annals . . . "[12]

The Texan army's total force had dwindled from a high of over 900 (after the Battle of Concepcion) to about 350 men. The Mexican forces, with their reinforcements, exceeded 1,500. The Texans lost four men killed and fifteen wounded. The Mexican losses were in excess of 150.[13] It should be remembered that Cos's army was made up partly by poorly trained soldiers, including a large number of convicts who had no desire to be heroes.

Johnson, Grant, and Fannin each added to their loyal followers during the siege and fall of Bexar. Each began an active campaign to mount expeditions to Matamoros.

After the Battle of Bexar

General Cos marched his army out of San Antonio after being defeated by the Texas volunteer army in early December of 1835 and reached the Rio Grande on Christmas Day. Two days later 1,500 men under Gen. Ramirez y Sesma arrived on the Rio Grande with orders from Santa Anna to go to San Antonio. At this point all Mexican troops were out of Texas; but Santa Anna was laying plans from his headquarters in San Luis Potosi for another incursion into Texas. Cos was told to go to Monclova and Ramirez y Sesma was directed to remain at San Juan Bautista on the Rio Grande, about eighty miles from Laredo.

With the fighting over in San Antonio many members of the volunteer army left for home. Col. Frank W. Johnson left for San Felipe to be honored by the council and to lobby for official approval for the Matamoros Expedition. Capt. Grant, after raiding the warehouses in Bexar, headed his troops to Goliad. Before leaving San Antonio Grant induced a number of men to join the Matamoros adventure.

5.

THE MATAMOROS EXPEDITION

Few things that occurred during the Texas Revolution affected decisions more than the Matamoros Expedition—an event that never actually took place.

The theory was quite simple: Strike a crippling blow to Mexico at Matamoros before they were able to bring armies into Texas. A simple proposition, but one that was fraught with the problems related to ego-inflated soldiers of fortune.

It is hard to pinpoint where the idea originated. It is safe to say that during the time when volunteers were amassed in Bexar in the fall of 1835 to deal with Gen. Martin Perfecto de Cos and his army, the idea turned into an armed expedition. The would-be leaders, who were all present in Bexar, began staking out their claims.

The Consultation, which convened in San Felipe on October 16, 1835, gave its approval for an expedition to Matamoros on November 13.[1] Philip Dimmitt, the commander at Goliad who was an early advocate of capturing Matamoros as a profit-making scheme, worked out a plan in November of 1835. He proposed to Gen. Stephen F. Austin capturing Matamoros for the port's revenue: "The port of Matamoros, if properly, and honestly superintended, would yield a very considerable revenue. At present, its income is said to be $100,000 per month. It is said that it ought to

produce much more. This is a formidable weapon." No record of
Dimmitt, or anyone else, following up on this money-making
scheme has ever been discovered.[2]

When the news of the victory over General Cos and the
Mexican army at Bexar on December 9, 1835, reached San Felipe,
the General Council drew up a memorial directed to the commanders, Gen. Edward Burleson and Col. F. W. Johnson, and their officers and men, full of praise for their bravery.[3] This was just the thing
that the promoters of the Matamoros Expedition needed to boost
their campaign. Colonel Johnson went to San Felipe and gave the
council an account of the action at Bexar. At the same time he
advanced his desires to head an expedition to Matamoros.

Colonel Johnson and Dr. James Grant had been playing both
ends against the middle. Backed by their troops, the two "generals"
did their best to strip the Bexar supply depots of all arms, ammunitions, and foods. They also "pressed" supplies of all types from private citizens in Bexar and continued this practice from settlers
between San Antonio and Goliad. When Grant arrived in Goliad
(Johnson having gone to San Felipe) he demanded, and received,
supplies from Dimmitt.[4]

Johnson, Grant, and Fannin each added to their loyal followers
during the siege and fall of Bexar. Each began work in earnest promoting their own Matamoros agenda when the shooting stopped.

Sam Houston, commander in chief of the Texas Army, jumped
into the middle of the Matamoros fray on December 17 when he
issued orders to James Bowie to "proceed on the route to
Matamoros, and, if possible reduce the place and retain possession
until further orders...." This idea was first advanced by the General
Council on November 13, and after hearing of Houston's order the
council went on record favoring General Houston to lead the expedition and so ordered. Since the order to Bowie was never finalized,
and Houston declined, these moves came to naught. By now
Houston appeared to have despaired over the conflicting policies of
the governor and the General Council. On December 30 Houston
addressed Gov. Henry Smith saying, "by the time I can hold an
Indian talk, and arrange matters for safety in the rear of the army ...
I will be ready, should there be the slightest necessity for my presence at Copano, or on the frontier, to repair instantly to the point

where I may be needed." With this Houston repaired to the Comanche Nation in East Texas where he understood the politics.[5]

Meanwhile, politics were boiling as the General Council began to assert itself as having equal power with Pres. Henry Smith.

On January 7, 1836, the council appointed J. W. Fannin and F. W. Johnson as agents "for carrying into effect the intended plan of operations in the descent upon Matamoros." Johnson withdrew from contention, for the moment, leaving the field open to Fannin.[6] Fannin immediately ran ads in Texas and United States newspapers inviting men to join him at Copano to form an army to take the war to Matamoros.

Dimmitt expanded even more on the feasibility of the Matamoros Expedition in a dispatch to General Houston that was published in the *Houston Telegraph and Register* on January 23, 1836:

> We have neither provoked, nor yet given cause for extending it [war] to Texas. It originated in the interior of the country [Mexico], in a contest for power, and there it belongs; and we owe it both to ourselves and the enemy, to carry it home. Let them have the war, and let us put them in a way to fight its battles. We can then remain a party to it, or withdraw, at pleasure, with honor enough, and with a well-earned enviable reputation. You will please urge this subject on the consideration of the Governor and Council with zeal, force, and untiring perseverance. Yours, respectfully, P. Dimmitt, Commandant.

Essentially, General Houston and Governor Smith saw the Matamoros Expedition as a way to stop the Mexican army before it had a chance to enter Texas and lay waste to homes of the settlers, and at the same time open the way for Texas to seek its own destiny. On the other hand it appeared that both Johnson and Grant wanted the expedition for their own glory and to aid the cause of the Federalists and not necessarily for the independence of Texas. Grant, it will be remembered, had extensive land holdings and other property in Coahuila and wanted to be restored to his property. Actually, the Mexicans in Texas who backed the Federalist movement wanted freedom from Coahuila, but not necessarily freedom from Mexico.

The Matamoros Expedition was rapidly approaching a breaking point. General Houston wrote to Governor Smith from headquarters in Goliad on January 17, 1836. He detailed the difficulties, and advised of the futility of a military expedition into enemy territory. Houston, as stated earlier, was a supporter of the project, but conditions and events evidently caused him to reconsider. He wrote to Governor Smith: "the army should not advance with a small force upon Matamoros with the hope, or belief, that the Mexicans will cooperate with us. I have no confidence in them and the Disaster at Tampico should teach us a lesson to be noted in our future operations."[7] In all likelihood Houston's support for the Matamoros Expedition vanished after Johnson, Fannin, and Grant began to compete for top billing and began plundering military warehouses in San Antonio and pressing supplies from private citizens.

Houston used this argument successfully when he addressed recruits who had gathered in January at Copano-Refugio to convince them not to participate in the expedition. The general's remarks are credited by most historians as causing Colonel Ward to take his men to Goliad to join Fannin rather than join the troops committed to the Matamoros Expedition. In a letter to Governor Smith on January 30 Houston noted with alarm the duplicity behind orders to Fannin from the General Council: "How was I to become acquainted with the orders of the Council? Was it through my subaltern? If he [Fannin] accepted any appointment incompatible with his obligation as a colonel in the regular army, it certainly increases his moral responsibilities to the extent which is truly to be regretted." It is small wonder that Houston sought the peace of a Cherokee village to sort out the conflict between the presidency and the General Council.[8]

The proposed Matamoros Expedition was a prime example of lack of direct lines of command and a supreme authority. As we shall see, these ingredients caused the young Republic to lose hundreds of gallant, young men.

It is interesting to note that the desire to mount an expedition did not end with the victory at San Jacinto. Shortly after the rout of Gen. Santa Anna, Col. Henry Wax Karnes and Henry Teal were sent to Matamoros to effect an exchange of prisoners being held there by the Mexicans. Instead of getting the release of the prisoners, Karnes was held. Then president of the Republic, David G. Burnet, and Gen. Thomas J. Rusk were planning an attack on the city by land and sea to free the prisoners. It never materialized and Karnes escaped shortly thereafter and returned to Texas to resume his command of a Ranger company. He died of yellow fever in San Antonio in 1842. Had he not died he was slated to lead the Santa Fe Expedition. Karnes County is named for the famous scout, Ranger, and pioneer.[9]

Another expedition against Matamoros was planned by Felix Huston when he was made junior brigadier general of the Texas army on a temporary basis by Gen. Sam Houston. For a short time he was commander in chief of the army. When Albert Sidney Johnson was sent to relieve Houston of his command, trouble ensued, resulting in a duel between the two men. The engagement was held on the Lavaca River, February 7, 1837, in which Johnson was seriously wounded. Huston continued his aggressive attitude against Mexico and proposed to plant a military colony of 5,000 to 10,000 men on the Rio Grande with himself as the leader. To finance the deal he proposed issuing $500,000 in bonds. The scheme did not meet General Houston's approval and died. He continued his interest in Texas and campaigned extensively in the South for approval of the annexation of Texas.[10]

Battle of San Patricio and Grant's Downfall

By January 15, 1836, Gen. Sam Houston had arrived at Refugio and called a mass meeting for all of the troops who had come by boat to Copano and others who had marched overland—all wanting a piece of the action against Mexico. By this time General Houston had dropped his support for the Matamoros Expedition, claiming it was not in the best interest of Texas. Only part of the general's speech has been found, but we know that Houston made a speech in an attempt to convince the men from joining any expedition headed for Matamoros. Houston stayed in the Copano-Refugio/Goliad area for almost a week and undoubtedly influenced the bulk of the soldiers not to join any Matamoros expedition.

When Col. James Fannin arrived in Refugio, Houston had already convinced a goodly portion of the troops gathered in the area not to go to Matamoros. Intelligence had also arrived about the growing strength of Mexican forces in Matamoros. With these facts in hand, Fannin opted to allow Col. Frank W. Johnson and Dr. James

Grant the dubious honor of heading the Matamoros Expedition. Fannin accepted the command of the fortress of La Bahia in Goliad, perhaps hoping a better opportunity would present itself later. On February 7 he was elected a colonel in the provisional regiment of volunteers for Goliad, and from February 12 to March 12 he was commander in chief of the army.[11]

Johnson had long been an advocate of a strike on Matamoros. In December of 1835 when he was a member of the Texan forces attacking Bexar, he wrote to the Committee of Military Affairs of the General Council setting out his agenda:

> I will make immediate arrangements for the expedition against Matamoros as we are fortunate enough to receive your recommendations to take such a step. It will, however, be necessary to await the arrival of reinforcements on the road to enable me to leave a sufficient garrison at this important point (Bexar). The difficulty which presents itself does not consist in a lack of volunteers, but on the contrary, persuading a sufficient number of garrison duty to remain behind. All wish to achieve new victories and to raise the glory of the army of Texas as well as to assist the friends of liberty in the interior in throwing off the yoke of tyranny.[12]

Making sure to touch all bases, Johnson wrote on Christmas Day to Lieutenant Governor Robinson, assuring him of his support for a Matamoros Expedition: "The expedition that you propose against Matamoros can be undertaken speedily with every rational prospect of success and every man in this garrison would willingly volunteer to proceed to the interior, but as the position [Bexar] which we occupy is all important to maintain, it will be desirable to await the arrival of considerable reinforcements...."[13]

Dr. James Grant, with about 200 Federalist volunteers, arrived in Goliad in early January and made camp in the ruins of the old Espiritu Santo Mission. On January 5, 1836, the arrogant Grant rode into the La Bahia fortress where the Bloody Arm flag of independence still waved over the walls, having been raised the day that the Goliad forces adopted a declaration of independence. Grant demanded that the flag be taken down, much to the chagrin of Commander Philip Dimmitt's forces, who bristled and armed themselves. Dimmitt kept his head and elected to lower the flag rather than pit his men against Grant's larger force, thus averting a bloody clash among Texans. Dimmitt also agreed to furnish the expedition with coffee, sugar, and a few other commodities from his meager supply. Not satisfied, the Freebooter came back with all of his force and took three cannons and the entire herd of horses that belonged personally to the men of the garrison. Dimmitt reported this seizure to the provisional government.[14]

Colonel Johnson, after leading the successful assault that crushed General Cos's army in Bexar, went to San Felipe and received just praise for his part in the victory. He lobbied the General Council for the authority to head an expedition to Matamoros, but even though their official support went to Fannin, he received enough encouragement that he left the seat of Texas government with plans to take Matamoros. He immediately marched with fifty followers and joined Grant and his force in the Goliad/Refugio area. All of the men evidently listened to a speech that General Houston delivered in which he withdrew his support for a Matamoros Expedition.

The forces of Colonel Johnson and Dr. Grant, numbering about seventy after a number of men decided to heed General Houston's advice, left the staging area around Refugio and arrived in San Patricio at the end of January. Upon arrival there they were informed that the former commander of Lipantitlan, Capt. Nicholas Rodriquez, was camped a short distance from the old colony settlement. Empresario James McGloin tells about this episode:

> Colonel Grant started with about 25 men to surprise him (Rodriquez), taking with him the person that gave the information, which was one of Rodriquez's own men. They got to the place at night, which was very late and found all fast asleep. On calling on them to surrender, or their lives would be taken if they resisted, They all answered ... they collected all their horses and marched them to San Patricio where they treated all well and took the commandant to their own quarters. In the course of three days they made their escape, no guard being placed over them....[15]

Another source tells that the Texans did not want prisoners, and so they freed them after receiving their pledge that they would not fight against Texas, a pledge that the Mexicans kept until they were able to rejoin Mexican forces. While at San Patricio, Daniel J. Toler, a partner of Colonel Grant in Coahuila who had just returned from Parras to check on their estates, reported that Santa Anna was at Saltillo with "eight or ten thousand men." This information was sent immediately to Colonel Fannin.

In order to get more horses to mount a cavalry force—a much needed adjunct for the Texan cause—the Matamoros Expedition traveled to the Santa Rosa Ranch near present-day Raymondville. This ranch later belonged to Charles F. Stillman who established a mercantile business in Matamoros in 1828.[16] After rounding up over one hundred horses Grant and Johnson began their return to San Patricio, visiting other ranches and getting all of the mounts that they could, sometimes buying them at a dollar a head. In later years when Johnson wrote a history of Texas he emphasized that they actually did buy part of the horses that they rounded up.

When about twenty miles from San Patricio, Grant learned that a number of horses and mules were a short distance below the road. Johnson argued that they had enough horses. More importantly, he was convinced that the enemy was being posted on their whereabouts. Grant prevailed and took his men and went in search of more horses. Johnson continued toward San Patricio, and when near the river he dispatched twelve men to take the horses to the ranch of Don Julian de la Garcia about four miles south of the city. Johnson and the remainder of the force crossed the river and went to San Patricio. Capt. Pearson and eight men camped in the public square, and the rest lodged in three different houses.[17]

Gen. Jose Urrea, through a network of spies, had kept track of the Johnson-Grant forces and left Matamoros with about 600 men when the Texans first arrived at San Patricio. Included in this force were 300 aborigines from the Yucatan who were inept in military training, and 230 dragoons, including several companies of convict-soldiers, and some infantrymen from scattered groups. In addition to this force about an equal number of camp followers—women and boys—trailed the troops. On February 25, 26, and 27, the poorly clad soldiers, who were used to a tropical climate, were exposed to a severely cold storm. This was probably a true Texas "norther." At least six soldiers died of exposure. General Urrea was notified at about 10 P.M. on February 26 by a scout that Johnson's force was now camped at San Patricio. The general immediately put his men into a forced march. Despite the harsh, cold, wet weather, Urrea's forces arrived at San Patricio about 3 A.M., February 27, 1836. He sent thirty men under Capt. Rafael Pretala to the ranch where the horses had been taken. In the attack that ensued four Texans were killed and eight taken prisoner.

In San Patricio Urrea's forces surrounded the houses where Johnson's men were sleeping. According to Urrea's report, sixteen Texans were killed and twenty-four taken prisoner in hand-to-hand fighting. Johnson and four men quartered with him managed to escape and made their way back to Goliad. Legend tells (confirmed by Urrea) that Urrea sent word ahead to the Irish settlers, who were loyal to Mexico, to leave a light burning in their homes and they would not be molested. It so happened that Johnson was working late—with a candle burning. Johnson, who later wrote a history book, put a different spin on the battle:

> On the second day after our arrival at San Patricio, we were sur-prised and attacked by Urrea's advance. After a short struggle, all were put to the sword, except Colonel Johnson, Daniel J. Toler, John H. Love of Georgia, and Miller of South Carolina. At the time we were rooming together, and had been joined by a Frenchman, a merchant of Matamoras. The house was soon sur-rounded, and an order given to open the door; there being no light in the house, the officer ordered a light to be made. Toler, who spoke the Castilian well, kept the officer in conversation while he pretended to be complying with the order. While thus engaged, fortunately for the inmates of the house, a fire was opened on the street in front, whether by a squad of their own men or by Texans is not known. This drew those in the rear of the house to the front. Apprised of this, Colonel Johnson gave the order to open the rear door, and to pass out, and escape if we could. The order was promptly obeyed; and the party escaped in safety to Goliad after some suffering and fatigue. The first night we stopped near Refugio, where we were joined by one of our companions—Beck, and by one or two at Goliad, who, like our-selves, had escaped from San Patricio.[18]

Historians put the total number of men with Johnson at about thirty-four—with eight killed, thirteen taken prisoner, and six escaping. At least seven Mexicans were with Johnson, with two being killed. Col. Jose Enrique de la Pena, an aide to Gen. Santa Anna, wrote in his diary that twenty were killed and thirty-two taken prisoner. Urrea wrote in his report that "the town and the

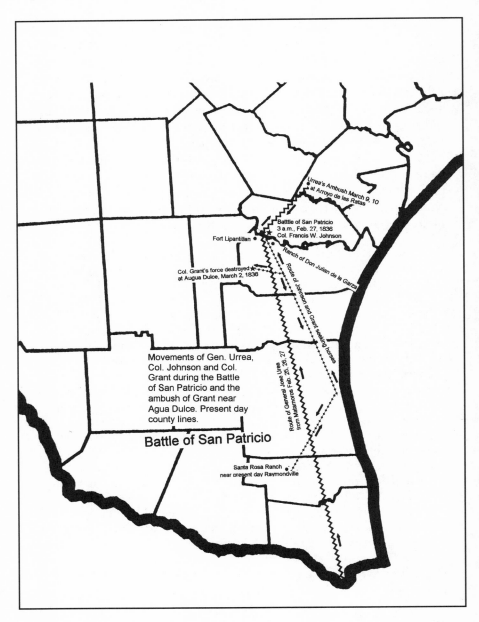

Urrea's Ambush March 9, 10
at Arroyo de las Ratas

Battle of San Patricio
3 a.m., Feb. 27, 1836
Col. Francis W. Johnson

Fort Lipantitlan

Ranch of Don Julian de la Garza

Col. Grant's force destroyed
at Augua Dulce, March 2, 1836

Route of Johnson and Grant stealing horses

Movements of Gen. Urrea,
Col. Johnson and Col.
Grant during the Battle
of San Patricio and the
ambush of Grant near
Agua Dulce. Present day
county lines.

Route of General Jose Urrea
from Matamoros Feb. 25, 26, 27

Battle of San Patricio

Santa Rosa Ranch
near present day Raymondville

Movements of General Urrea, Colonel Johnson, and Colonel Grant during the Battle of San Patricio and the ambush of Grant near Agua Dulce. Present-day county lines.

rest of the inhabitants did not suffer the least damage." In his account of the action Empresario James McGloin commented that "Johnson's quarters was surrounded and he was asked to surrender by the enemy which was in front of his place. He was answered from within by Mr. Daniel Toler a partner of Colonel Grant who came a few days before from the interior of Mexico that he would surrender, but at the same time opened the back of his tent and got to Mission of Refugio next day 12 A.M. without hat, shoes or Coat."

McGloin reported that the Texans were buried the next day by "the Rev. T. J. Malloy in the Church yard." Other residents of San Patricio say that the burial was in the old cemetery on the hill and it was here that the state placed a marker in 1986 commemorating those who died at the Battle of San Patricio.[19]

The Mexican army remained in San Patricio until its spies brought word that Grant was on the march toward San Patricio. On March 2 Urrea's men ambushed Grant's party near a Banquete Creek crossing close to present-day Agua Dulce. Grant and all men, except six who escaped, were killed or captured. General Urrea had sent two of his spies to contact Grant the day before, telling him that, "Colonel Johnson and his party was well and expecting him [Grant] momentarily." McGloin described the battle: "When he [Grant] got himself enclosed by such superior forces, being there was no way to escape he told the men [to hold their] ground and fight until killed, the enemy not giving [them] time to look by rushing on to them separated them ..." Colonel Grant ran his horse seven miles before he was overtaken and lanced. Historian Harbert Davenport lists twelve killed, four captured, and six escaped. The fallen men were stripped of weapons and clothing and were left naked on the battlefield. One account tells that Reverend Malloy went to the battlefield and brought the bodies to San Patricio; however, other reports tell of the bodies being left where they had fallen and eventually most of the bones were scattered by wild animals.

Probably the best account of Grant's ambush was written by R. R. Brown, a member of Grant's squadron who was captured. Part of the firsthand account follows:

> Our party started out on another expedition immediately, going north of the road to Matamoras. On the second day out a Mexican fell in with us, pretending that he wished to join us, and that he could bring with him a small Mexican company of

mounted men. We suspected him for a spy, and our suspicions were confirmed in the morning when we found he had left during the night ... having taken a considerable number of horses. We returned on our way back to San Patricio, visiting the different ranches, getting the horses we could, and sometimes buying them at a dollar a head. We had reached the Agua Dulce [creek], within some twenty miles of San Patricio, and, in high spirits, we made an early start from that place, Colonel Grant, Placido Benavides and myself being about a half a mile ahead to lead the horses, and the rest of the company following ... suddenly there came out from each of these motts several hundred Mexican dragoons, who quickly closed in, surrounding both the horses and our party. Grant, Placido and myself might then have made our escape, as we were well mounted and some distance in advance; but our first impulse being to relieve our party ... Grant persuaded Placido to start forthwith for Goliad, and give Fannin information about Urrea's return ... Grant and myself finding ourselves the only survivors of our party ... after we had run six or seven miles, they surrounded us ... I felt myself fast in a lasso that had been thrown over me ... After Grant fell I saw some ten or a dozen officers go up and run their sword through his body.

Brown was held in captivity for a number of months before he and McNeely escaped and finally made their way back to Texas.

It took a long time for news of the crushing defeat of Johnson and Grant to reach the outside world. On Saturday, March 12, 1836 (two weeks after the Battle of San Patricio) the *Houston Telegraph and Register* reported in a small note: "It is reported that Colonel Johnson's party, who went to the west, were surprised, and all, with the exception of himself and two or three others, killed by the Mexicans. Colonel Grant is not heard of."

General Urrea stayed camped near San Patricio until March 12. On the 7th a section of his force that had remained at Matamoros joined him, and he spent several days disciplining them and making the men carry out continuous exercises. When he left he took the cattle and horses gathered by Grant and Johnson, as well as their arms and ammunition. The battle scene would now shift to Refugio/Goliad.[20]

6.

GOLIAD/REFUGIO
CAMPAIGNS

Few individuals have been so enshrined into Texas history as Col. James Walker Fannin, Jr. At the same time, few have had their judgment questioned as much by historians. But Colonel Fannin was not alone when it came to judgment calls, as we shall see.

Col. James Walker Fannin, Jr., was born on a Georgia plantation, perhaps as an illegitimate scion of one of the state's oldest families. He entered West Point at the age of fourteen, using the name of his maternal grandfather, J. W. Walker, but after less than two years returned home. His cousin, Martha Fannin, says that he left West Point due to a fight.[1] After his marriage to Minerva Fort, and the birth of two daughters, the family moved to Texas, settling near Velasco. He evidently operated a sugar plantation and was a slave owner, trader, and a Mason.[2] He was active in revolutionary affairs in the early 1830s and appeared in Gonzales as captain of the Brazos guards. He was prominent in the Battle of Concepcion in San Antonio (October 28, 1835) with James Bowie. He was also present for the siege of San Antonio de Bexar on December 11. On November 13 Gen. Sam Houston named Fannin inspector general of the army with the rank of colonel. After serving with distinction in the volunteer army, Fannin was commissioned in the regular army by General Houston on December 7, 1835. Early in 1836 he

began actively recruiting men for a proposed invasion of Matamoros, having received permission from the military committee of
the General Council to undertake the expedition with Frank
Johnson. When Houston withdrew his support for the Matamoros
Expedition, Fannin was elected to be a colonel of the provisional
regiment of volunteers at Goliad. Historian Clarence Wharton
theorized that Fannin was not willing to march with Johnson and
Grant. Soldiers noted that there was ill feeling between Grant and
Fannin.[3]

During December a number of volunteer groups arrived in
Texas in response to a call for help publicized in the United States.
Among these were the Georgia Battalion, the Alabama (Mobile)
Greys, Westover Company, San Antonio Greys, Tampico Blues,
Paducah Volunteers, Kentucky Riflemen (Mustangs), and Mata-
gorda Volunteers. Others who eventually landed at Port Copano in
December and January and joined Colonel Fannin's command
included: Red Rovers (organized by Dr. Jack Shackelford, Ala-
bama); Capt. John C. Grace's Squad; Lt. Samuel Sprague's Squad;
Refugio Militia Co., under Capt. Hugh McDonald Fraser; Capt.
A. C. Horton's Company of Matagorda Volunteers; men who
escaped from the Grant/Johnson expedition; and a scattering of
volunteers from Pennsylvania, New York, Massachusetts, and New
Hampshire.[4]

Colonel Fannin, after receiving a grant of power to act as an
agent for the provisional government of Texas on January 7, caused
this advertisement to run in papers in Texas and the United States:

ATTENTION VOLUNTEERS:

To the west, face: March
An expedition to the west has been ordered by the General
Council, and the volunteers from Bexar, Goliad, Velasco, and else-
where, are ordered to rendezvous at San Patricio, between the
24th and 27th, inst. and report to the officer in command. The
fleet convoy will sail from Velasco under my charge, on or about
the 18th, and all who feel disposed to join it, and aid in keeping
the war out of Texas, and at the same time cripple the enemy in
their resources at home, are invited to enter the ranks forthwith.

J. W. FANNIN, Jr.[5]
January 8th, 1836

Fannin arrived at Port Copano on February 1, 1836, on the *Flora*. The *Columbus*, *Laura*, and *Liberty* also landed troops and supplies during this period. Fannin proceeded to Refugio, arriving on February 5, and immediately began regimental organization. He was elected colonel and William Ward was made lieutenant colonel. Other officers included: J. M. Chadwich, captain adjutant; and John Sowers Brooks, captain assistant adjutant and aide. Fannin reported to Provisional Governor Robinson that there were about 400 men in the area, with "less than twenty-five native Texans." In his army communications to Robinson, Fannin suggested that if Houston failed to return that he would take charge of the army. Houston became disillusioned over the inability of the president and the General Council to work together. As a result, he left to spend some time with the Indians in deep East Texas in an attempt to keep out of the war. Robinson, who took over as acting governor when Gov. Henry Smith was removed from office by the General Council, evidently did not give Fannin any encouragement in his quest to be put in charge of all forces fighting in Texas.[6]

At the time that Fannin landed at Copano there were already a number of men from all over Texas in and around Refugio. In fact, on February 1, 1836, the citizens of the Refugio municipality opened polls to elect two delegates to the convention set for March 1 in San Felipe. By consensus the citizens had decided to send Empresario James Power and Gen. Sam Houston as delegates. When the polls opened a number of soldiers presented themselves to vote, and after a hasty huddle, the election judges refused the soldiers the right to vote on the grounds that they were not citizens of the municipality. The troops then held their own election and sent Samuel A. Maverick and Jesse B. Badgett as their representatives and sent a memorial to the convention, signed by all of the soldiers, complaining of not being allowed to vote. The same thing happened in San Patricio where James McGloin had the soldiers apply for a headright to make them legal to vote, which they did. When the election judges found out that the soldiers were not voting for the local choices, their ballots were thrown out. John Bower and John McMullen, both colonists, were elected.[7]

Fannin Heads for Goliad

Fannin's company moved out of Refugio on February 12-13, arriving at Fort La Bahia on the 14th. Fannin's resolve as a commander was tested when Col. James Butler Bonham arrived in Goliad on February 25 with an urgent appeal from William Travis, commander at the Alamo, for immediate relief from the pressure of General Santa Anna's forces, which had drawn up before the old fort. Fannin issued orders for a relief column of about 300 men to march immediately to the Alamo, leaving Capt. Ira Westover in Goliad with a small force to look after La Bahia. Fannin explained his predicament in an official letter dated February 29: "I have to report, that yesterday, after making all the preparations possible, we took up our line of march toward Bexar to the relief of those brave

Oldest known photo of La Bahia Presidio, Goliad, Texas, circa 1860.
—Photo courtesy Institute of Texan Cultures.

men now shut up in the Alamo, and to raise the siege . . . Within two hundred yards of town, one of the wagons broke down and it was necessary to double teams in order to draw the artillery across the river . . ." While stewing over this problem it was brought to his attention that, "not a particle of breadstuff, with the exception of half a measure of rice, with us—no beef, with the exception of a small portion which had been dried—and not a head of cattle . . ." Fannin called for a council of war of all commissioned officers and they unanimously counseled to turn back. An express was sent to Gonzales to let the committee of safety there know of his change in plans.

Another factor that influenced the decision to turn back was the information that had been brought into camp by Col. John White Bower, Fannin's chief spy, who brought the stark news that a Mexican advance was eminent and that Goliad could expect an attack soon.[8]

Perhaps trying to understand Colonel Fannin's action, Gen. Sam Houston reflected on the colonel's action: "at one time, [he] had taken up the line of march for the Alamo, but the breaking down of a wagon induced him to fall back, and abandon the idea of marching to the relief of our last hope in Bexar. Since then, he has written letters here, indicating a design to march upon San Patricio, and also the occupation of Copano . . . I am at a loss to know where my express will find him."[9]

Actually, Fannin did entertain, at least for a short time, carrying out a somewhat bizarre attack on San Patricio and General Urrea. The idea was presented to Fannin by Capt. Jesus Comanche Cuellar, an officer in Cos's army who had deserted and guided Ben Milam and his force in their successful attack at Bexar. His reward was a commission in the Texas cavalry. Comanche proposed to go to Urrea, who was camped at San Patricio, and plead that he had repented, and to prove his sincerity he would tell the general that Fannin was preparing a strike at San Patricio. Urrea bought into the scheme and actually took a force of 300 men on a northerly road to Goliad and camped at the Arroyo de las Ratas on March 8-10 and prepared an ambush for Fannin. In Urrea's diary he wrote: "March 8, I was informed that the enemy was taking steps to attack me in San Patricio. I marched during the night to meet them. . . . Ten leagues from Goliad I ambushed my troops on the road to await the enemy. March 9: In ambush on the Ratas Creek. March 10: I received news that the enemy had changed its plan . . ." The validity of the scheme is borne out by Gen. Vicente Filisola, who reported that Comanche told Urrea that "the rebels had decided to come to attack." Fannin was one up on both conspirators— he had backed out of the scheme, probably due to the increased pressure in Refugio.

General Urrea notes in his *diario* on March 8, 9, and 10, taking 300 men on the ambush attempt, and returning to San Patricio on March 11. As planned, Fannin was supposed to strike at the diminished force in San Patricio, and, after destroying them, march and surprise Urrea from the rear. Fannin evidently passed this information on to Houston, causing the general still another headache. Comanche left Urrea's force on March 9, telling the general: "I will lead Fannin into your trap . . ." Comanche finished the war with Texan forces and made his home in Goliad.[10]

As the days passed and news of General Urrea's approaching army became more pressing, Fannin abandoned Port Copano as an outpost after inspecting Cox's Point and Dimmitt's Landing on Lavaca Bay as possible points where supplies could be landed. It will be remembered that Houston based his defense strategy on controlling Port Copano, knowing that the Mexicans would have a difficult time supplying their armies overland. Lt. Col. Enrique Pena, aide to General Santa Anna, also advocated transporting troops to Texas by boat. He reasoned that armies traveling overland from Mexico would bring a large number of camp followers, thus alleviating the problem of supplies. The advance of General Urrea's army, coming overland from Matamoros, caused Fannin to rethink this procedure and consider ports in Lavaca Bay. It is ironic that Fannin's command at Goliad ran low on food despite the fact that the *Caroline* brought in a large amount of supplies at Cox's Point (near present-day Port Lavaca). Lack of wagons kept the needed food from getting to the soldiers at La Bahia. Not only was the food supply critical, but it was now necessary for the Texas high command to reconsider the strategic importance of Goliad, since they could not control the Mexicans' use of Port Copano as a troop disembarkation point. Victoria began to look like an easier place to defend than Goliad. On March 1 Fannin wrote to the acting government seeking an order to retreat from Goliad.[11]

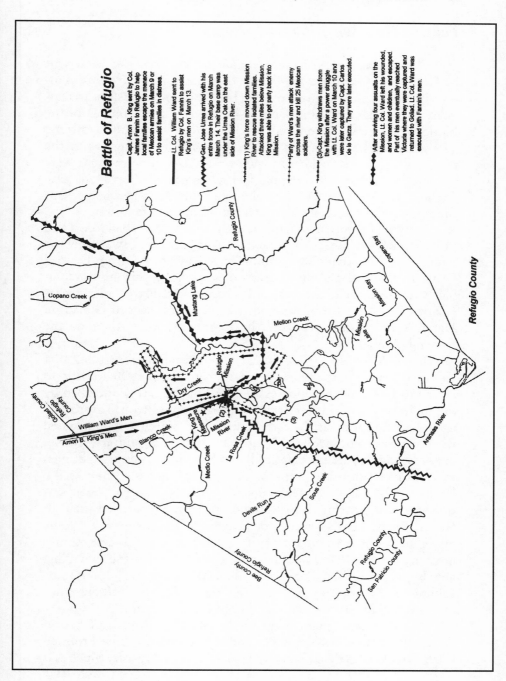

Battle of Refugio

— Capt. Amon B. King sent by Col. James Fannin to Refugio to help local families escape the menace of Mexican armies on March 9 or 10 to assist families in distress.

— Lt. Col. William Ward sent to Refugio by Col. Fannin to assist King's men on March 13.

〰️ Gen. Jose Urrea arrived with his entire force in Refugio on March March 14. Their base camp was under the Urrea Oak on the east side of Mission River.

⁃⁃⁃⁃ (1) King's force moved down Mission River to rescue isolated families. Attacked three miles below Mission, King was able to get party back into Mission.

+++++ Party of Ward's men attack enemy across the river and kill 25 Mexican soldiers.

++++ (3) Capt. King withdraws men from the Mission after a power struggle with Lt. Col. Ward on March 10 and were later captured by Capt. Carlos de la Garza. They were later executed.

◆◆◆◆ After surviving four assaults on the Mission, Lt. Col. Ward left his wounded, and women and children, and escaped. Part of his men eventually reached Victoria where they were captured and returned to Goliad. Lt. Col. Ward was executed with Fannin's men.

Fannin Gets Warning

Placido Benavides, former *alcalde* of Victoria, had been sent by Col. James Grant to warn Fannin of the arrival of Urrea just minutes before Grant's men were slaughtered in an ambush near Banquete. Benavides arrived in Goliad shortly after the survivors of the Battle of San Patricio arrived.[12] While pacing the floor worrying about General Urrea, Fannin put his men to work strengthening the fort's fortifications, making it ready for a siege. Nine cannons were mounted in the walls and the old fort was renamed "Fort Defiance." Fannin has been criticized for rebuilding the fort when he perhaps should have been training his green troops in the arts of war.[13]

Colonel Fannin must have thought that he was abandoned and isolated in South Texas as General Urrea pressed forward. In the afternoon of February 28 Fannin received an express from Edward Gritten telling of the destruction of Colonel Johnson's force at old San Patricio. Gritten was collector of the district of Aransas (Copano). Colonel Johnson and five survivors reached Goliad on March 1 and Fannin reported the facts as he knew them to the General Council.

Lewis Ayers, Refugio colonist, brought news on March 2 that his and other Refugio families were unprotected at Refugio with no means to flee with their possessions. All of the carts controlled by the military at Goliad were transporting supplies from Lavaca Bay to Goliad.[14] As soon as the carts returned on March 9, Fannin acted with compassion, probably without assessing military consequences, and dispatched Capt. William King with twenty-eight men and part of Bradford's company, plus wagons, to assist the Refugio families' flight from Urrea's advance. King's men had been stationed at the old church in Refugio until Fannin recalled them to Goliad when Travis's request for help at the Alamo arrived.[15] Some historians wonder whether Fannin realized that he was setting into motion an event that would become a battle cry for the struggling new Republic. Others ponder why he allowed his small force to be splintered. And still others seek the reason for the Refugio colonists staying in harms' way, refusing to leave their homes.

As soon as Captain King was recalled to Goliad on February 25, Refugio was completely undefended on the Raw Frontier. Capt. Don Carlos de la Garza and his Victoriana Guards, which was composed of a number of Mexican rancheros and a band of sympathetic Indians, rode into town on February 27, making life dangerous for the Refugio colonists. Into this troubled setting the survivors of the Battle of San Patricio straggled late on the 28th with their tales of horror. Garza and his rancheros rode on to San Patricio to confer with General Urrea, leaving behind the Indians to plunder and ransack the stores and homes in Refugio. The bulk of Refugio men were serving in the military: some with Ira Westover, various units in Fannin's army, two at the Alamo, some with Sam Houston's regulars, and others on special duty. Most of the remaining men were members of Fraser's Militia which was active in scouting and spy work and away from home most of the time.[16]

King Returns to Refugio

Captain King and his relief company arrived in Refugio probably on March 10 or 11 and learned that the Ayers family and others were still at their ranches down the Mission River. Leaving some carts in town to be loaded, King's men headed out to pick up the settlers along the river. In the process they had to beat off an attack by a small band of rancheros and Karankawa Indians who harassed the relief caravan, but they finally reached the safety of the mission fort ruins. King lost three men in the running skirmish. One soldier was wounded and one of the women rescued had been shot in the leg. Since Capt. Carlos de la Garza and a sizeable force of rancheros and Indians were in Refugio, Captain King decided that he would be unable to get the slow-moving carts back to Goliad without help. He sent word to Fannin asking for reinforcements. The messenger arrived at Goliad near midnight on the 11th. It should be remembered that the rancheros were General Urrea's eyes and ears, and as events transpired riders who kept an accurate chart on the whereabouts of all of Fannin's forces hurried to report to Urrea.[17]

Colonel Fannin did not hesitate—he immediately ordered Lieutenant Colonel Ward to take his Georgia Battalion, plus a few others, and go to the relief of King. Estimates as to the number of men run from 120 to 150. They left Goliad about 3 A.M. on March 13, arriving in Refugio about 2 P.M. to find Captain King surrounded in the ruins of the old church by 200 to 300 Mexicans. In the ensuing action the attackers were routed, and forced to cross to the other side of the Mission River.[18]

It was Lieutenant Colonel Ward's plan to return immediately to Goliad; however, the best laid plans sometimes go awry. His men were tired after marching all day and some of them had built up a lot of frustration against the Mexicans. Captain Ticknor, with some of his and Bradford's men, crossed the Mission River in the night and blasted the Mexican camp, killing at least eight. Not satisfied with their night escapade, they returned the next morning to savor their work, flushing Mexican soldiers carrying off their dead. They helped themselves to the Mexicans' horses before returning to Refugio.[19]

Trouble between Ward and King broke out the next morning. Captain King insisted that by being first on the scene he should take command. Lieutenant Colonel Ward stood firm on his rank as senior and in charge. Like a thwarted school boy, King took his men, as well as about twenty of Captain Bradford's, and left the old church and went to Esteban Lopez's ranch to capture Lopez.[20] Still another version of this incident has King leaving after the dispute to do some scouting, after which he would return to the mission.[21] In either scenario it is obvious that the commanders thought more of their rank than the well-being of their men.

Captain King did leave the mission on March 14 with as many as fifty men. He burned Lopez's ranch house and several others, and when he attempted to return to Refugio he was attacked by a large Mexican force, causing him to take refuge along the river bank about a mile south of Refugio. Repeated attempts to dislodge the Texans failed and during the night they managed to cross the river. They were on their way to Goliad when they were captured and returned to the mission on March 15. Ward's forces had left the mission after midnight the previous morning.[22]

When General Urrea unleashed his attack on Ward's men at the mission on March 14, there were a number of women and children from the colony and about twenty captured local Mexicans also within the fort's walls. Ward, seeing the odds that he faced, sent Edward Perry with a message to Fannin asking for reinforcements and ammunition. Perry returned to Ward bringing word that General Houston had ordered a retreat to Victoria and Ward was instructed to disengage himself and return to Goliad.[23] Four assaults were carried out by the Mexicans with heavy losses. In the afternoon, after a heavy artillery bombardment, Urrea's entire army was now in place, and the Mexicans launched another attack about 4 P.M. Failing to overwhelm the Texans, the attackers drew back at nightfall, ringing the mission with squads who lighted bonfires. Knowing that he must get back to Goliad, Ward passed the word that the wounded would have to be left behind with the women and children. Two Texans volunteered to remain with them—Samuel Wood and William K. Simpson.[24] Just before Ward's forces left the mission, Perry Davis, one of King's men, managed to get into the mission. He advised Ward not to travel the main road since it was well guarded.

At General Houston's headquarters in Gonzales the general was totally in the dark as to what was going on in Refugio/Goliad. On March 13 the general sent a dispatch to James Collinsworth, chairman of the military committee, in which he reviewed his lack of communication with Colonel Fannin and emphasized his belief that "with our small, unorganized force, we cannot maintain sieges in fortresses, in the country of the enemy . . ." Houston had sent a dispatch on March 11 advising Fannin of the fall of the Alamo, but he had no way of knowing the predicament now facing Fannin.

Ward's Men Break Out

Ward and his men were successful in slipping out between two of the fires that ringed the mission. After securing water for the mission's wounded, they made an effort to go toward Copano.[25] James H. Neeley, a member of Ward's force who survived the ordeal, described what happened next. The story was published in the *Houston Telegraph and Register* on September 30, 1836.

Under cover of the darkness of the hour, (past midnight) the Texans succeeded in withdrawing from the church, undetected by the Mexicans, leaving behind them their wounded, who, with King and his men, prisoners, were next morning taken out by the dastard, sanguinary foe, tied and shot. Ward reached Victoria on the 23rd, and there fell in with the Mexican division to which Fannin had just surrendered, and he took to the woods, continuing his march about twelve miles from Victoria, when he found himself again encompassed by the enemy. When in this predicament he was informed by one of Capt. Guerra's company (an ex-friendly Mexican, who had joined the enemy) that Dimmitt's Landing, on the La Baca, was only two miles distant, and he sent two men to ascertain the fact, but they were captured and one was sent back by the enemy to offer the same terms of capitulation as they had granted to Fannin. Worn out with fatigue, and destitute of provisions and ammunitions, Ward saw no other alternative than to accept the offer, and afterwards was included with his party in the massacre of Fannin and his division. Sixteen of Col. Ward's men, who after their capture had been detailed by the enemy for labor, made their escape, of whom our narrator, James H. Neeley, was one. Distance from Goliad to Mission del Refugio, in Power's Colony, fifteen miles.

On the morning of March 15 when Urrea discovered that the Texans had left the mission, he ordered soldiers to enter. The wounded and their caretakers were bayoneted unmercifully. The women and children were not molested, partially due to a Mexican prisoner by the name of Cobian who interceded on their behalf. Mrs. Scott and three other Refugio women were able to smuggle critically wounded Abraham Osborne out of the mission between two mattresses without detection. Later Mrs. Osborne asked General Urrea to come to the home where her husband was taken, which he did. She tackled the problem head-on, saying, "My husband is in this house—I fear he is wounded mortally. I beg you to save him from the fury of your soldiers." Urrea requested to see the wound that was made by a one-ounce round ball that went completely through his body. Urrea sent his surgeon to treat the man and continued treating the enemy with compassion for as long as his army was in Refugio.

In a similar act, the life of Lewis Ayers was saved when Mrs. Ayers intervened with General Urrea. Ayers made the Masonic sign, which Urrea saw and ordered Ayers not to be shot. Several men with German names were saved from the firing squad by Col. J. J. Holsinger, a German who was an officer in the Mexican army.

On March 16 thirty of King's men were marched out on the Bexar-Goliad road and shot by General Urrea's explicit order: "I authorized the execution, after my departure from camp, of thirty adventurers taken prisoners." Their bleached bones remained on the prairie long after the revolution ended. The final resting place of these heroes was lost until May 9, 1944, when bones were discovered in a new grave that was being opened in the Mount Calvary Cemetery in Refugio. Further investigation by Father William H. Oberste and J. Frank Low, a local archeologist, uncovered the bones of sixteen men. Bullets in the bodies and skulls, as well as military relics, buttons, etc., were discovered to identify the bodies. With special permission a requiem mass was said on June 17, 1944. Legends say that there were actually thirty-two men who were shot with the other sixteen being buried in a grave located in a hackberry mott behind the cemetery. General Urrea rationalized shooting the prisoners in this manner: "I found myself threatened from El Copano, Goliad, and Victoria . . . I was overcome by the difficult circumstances that surrounded me. I authorized the execution . . . of thirty adventurers."[26]

The effectiveness of Mexican spies was highlighted in the Refugio/Goliad Campaign. Local rancheros, probably numbering as many as 200, were the eyes of the Mexican army, as well as scouts, and at times, actual combatants. As noted, the rancheros in the vicinity of Goliad, led by Capt. Don Guadalupe de los Santos, gradually pulled their families out of Goliad and moved to their ranches on the San Antonio River. During the time when some of Ward and King's units tried to escape to either Victoria or Goliad, it was these rancheros who hunted them and brought them in to be executed. Juan and Augustin Moya of Goliad were two of the best scouts for this type of work. Others who played important roles in feeding information to the Mexican army included Capt. Carlos de la Garza Sabriego, Padre Valdez, Capt. Carlos de la Garza (Victoriana Guardes), Goliad *alcalde* Encarnacion Galan, and Don Juan Antonio de los Santos. As mentioned earlier, at various times Karankawa Indians joined the rancheros, and their familiarity with the territory was especially useful in tracking down the stragglers from the Battle of Refugio.[27]

Fannin's Precarious Position

While Col. James Fannin kept vigil at Fort Defiance he had plenty of time to contemplate on his short, but turbulent career that ran from West Point through the Brazos River bottoms, to the intrigue and politics of the Texas military in late 1835, and the first three months of 1836. Ambitious for military glory, Fannin sought and obtained authorization to mount a strike against Matamoros. As forces from the United States began arriving at Port Copano, it appeared that Fannin's day had arrived. When Gen. Sam Houston entered the scene and addressed the eager soldiers, he convinced most of them that a strike against Matamoros would be foolish. Fannin, in all probability, reached an understanding with Dr. Grant and Colonel Johnson that called for Grant and Johnson to move on to San Patricio and Fannin to go to Goliad, both to refine their plans.[28]

With the Texas army lacking a true line of authority, coupled with the feuding of the General Council with President Smith, the outlook for Texas was bleak. Santa Anna had his main army of over one thousand men at San Juan Bautista on the Rio Grande headed for San Antonio where Col. James Clinton Neill watched and waited in the Alamo. When Colonel Travis relieved Neill on February 14, 1836, the total troops stood at about 200. General Urrea was poised at Matamoros with more than 600 men, preparing to move against Grant and Johnson with their less than one hundred troops. Mexican spies kept reporting on Fannin and his men scattered in Refugio and Goliad. The Mexican forces marched to a single drum beat—Santa Anna's. The Texas army had an ear for the General Council, another for the president and vice president, and listened with both to the clamoring of would-be generals for support for their self-serving agendas.[29] Santa Anna and Urrea had reason to be a bit cocky as they headed north.

Stripped of the King and Ward commands, Colonel Fannin was in trouble. He had a total of about 302 men left in his command.

When General Houston arrived in Gonzales on March 11, after the fall of the Alamo on March 6, 1836, one of his first actions was to send an order to Fannin at Goliad to fall back immediately to Victoria. Fannin, after giving consideration to the fact that the fate of King and Ward were hanging in the balance, replied that he had "held a council of war and determined to defend the place." Fannin had taken the responsibility to disobey an order from Gen. Sam Houston.[30]

Fannin Prepares to Abandon Fort Defiance

When Gen. Jose Urrea finished licking his wounds and mopping up after the Refugio battles, he headed for Goliad with just over 900 men. He left Col. Rafael de la Varga at Refugio to watch over a supply depot and hospital that he had set up. The colonel was also to keep a watchful eye on any movement of men or supplies at Port Copano. Just as important to his operation, he spread out his network of spies (rancheros) along the road from Refugio to Goliad. The results were quick when one outrider intercepted a communication from Col. James Fannin to Col. William Ward. The dispatch was to alert Ward that Fannin was abandoning Fort Defiance and heading for Victoria. Fannin had no way of knowing that the forces of King and Ward had been destroyed. Urrea immediately sent word to Capt. Mariano Iraeta, who had sixty men in the vicinity of Goliad, to take up a position that would straddle Fannin's escape route to Victoria.[31]

While Fannin was "bottled up" in La Bahia, Gen. Sam Houston was staying a step ahead of General Santa Anna's army. Houston's thoughts were with the men at Goliad. From his camp on the Navidad on March 15 Houston addressed a letter to Chairman Collinsworth[32] in which he noted: "I am fearful Goliad is besieged by the enemy. My order to Colonel Fannin, directing the place to be blown up, the cannon to be sunk in the river, and to fall back on Victoria, would reach him before the enemy could advance . . . ." In fact, Fannin did receive the order on March 13, according to historian John Henry Brown,[33] but did not begin the retreat until March 19—six days later. On March 17 Houston sent Fannin still another message telling him to fall back to Lavaca Bay to either Cox's Point or Dimmitt's Landing.[34] Fannin never got this message as this was the day his force finally left Goliad.

Fannin had sent three messengers[35] to Refugio for news about the situation. All had fallen into the hands of the enemy. Finally, on

March 16 Capt. Hugh McDonald Fraser, a Refugio colonist who was familiar with the territory, volunteered to ride out and bring back an accurate assessment. He returned in the afternoon of the 17th with the news that the Refugio detachment had been wiped out. Fannin immediately sent out Capt. Albert C. Horton's cavalry unit to find the enemy troops. He returned to report that troops that he estimated at 1,500 were approaching (Colonel Morales was on his way to reinforce Urrea.). Fannin began immediately to make preparations to leave. He destroyed a large part of the town of La Bahia by fire and battering ram.

When morning came on March 18, enemy troops were spotted nearby. Horton's cavalry chased the enemy, only to have them get reinforcements and fight back, causing him to retreat to the old mission across the river from La Bahia. The fort's artillery, plus a squad of Red Rovers, forced the enemy to retire.[36]

Everything had been made ready during the night to move out at dawn. The oxen were in place with loaded carts and the men at ready. When the diversion put things on hold, no one remembered the oxen who stood without food and water all morning. Finally, it was decided to pull out under the cover of darkness. Horton's cavalry was sent out to scout and returned with the word that Mexican troops were lying in wait across the river at the fort. The night retreat was canceled and rescheduled for dawn. Dr. J. H. Barnard wrote in his journal: "we were by no means disposed to run. We confidently counted on our ability to take ourselves and all our baggage, to safety in Victoria." Barnard's confidence came from the fact that Fannin's force still had about 270 men, plus about thirty of Colonel Horton's cavalry, which they reasoned would be enough to fight their way to Victoria.

It was after 9 A.M. on March 19 before the movement of men and materials actually got started under cover of a dense fog. Artillery that was not to be taken was spiked, and foodstuffs that could not be carried were burned. The Red Rovers were in the front, with Duval's Mustangs acting as the rear guard.[37]

While the life-and-death drama was being played out in Goliad, the convention at Washington-on-the-Brazos was struggling to get the new republic started. It decided that the first president, vice president, and cabinet would be named by the convention. On

March 18 David G. Burnet was named president "ad interim" over Samuel P. Carson by a majority of seven votes.[38]

SNAFU[39] is supposed to have been coined in modern days, but anything that could go wrong, did go wrong in these early hours of the retreat. A cannon was lost in the river and had to be fished out with brute strength; oxcarts broke down; oxen were unmanageable; food for the troops had been left behind, except for what each soldier carried; chests filled with muskets were dumped because of weight—the road was littered with everything imaginable; confusion reigned. Things seemed to improve as the army crossed the Manahuilla Creek and stopped at a patch of green grass to allow the tiring oxen a chance to graze. Horton's cavalry was instructed to cover the rear and flanks and report immediately any enemy troops. They reported no men in sight. After an hour the column took up the march and topped a small ridge when they saw Mexican infantry and cavalry in a belt of trees up ahead. Four cavalry scouts who had been out in front to detect the enemy had grown weary and dismounted to take a nap. A cannon shot fired by Fannin at the Mexicans fell short of its mark, but did awaken the lookouts.[40] The help expected from the cavalry by Dr. Barnard proved to be nonexistent. In fact, the four mounted men, evidently alarmed, sped past the Texans and only one, a German by the name of Herman Ehrenburg, joined Fannin's men. The others disappeared in the distance.

After a short time Fannin gave the order to advance toward the timber, which now appeared alive with Mexican soldiers. Fannin had the artillery drop back, and the troops formed a hollow square with lines three deep as they all moved slowly forward toward the Mexicans. John C. Duval later wrote: "I thought there were at least ten thousand, but in reality there were about a thousand besides several hundred infantry."[41]

Battle Joined on Prairie

The exhausted oxen pulling the carts and wagons began reacting to the confusion. They balked, refusing to move forward. Some had been killed by the fast moving Mexican cavalry, but regardless, several carts and wagons had to be abandoned as Fannin's force sought to assume a defensive posture on a "commanding eminence" on the prairie.[42] The die was cast when the ammunition cart broke down and it was necessary to rearrange the hollow square with the ammunition wagon in the middle. Survivors describe the battle-grounds as being in a slight depression. Timber, or cover, was in the distance: In front there was timber on Coleto Creek about one mile, in the rear was timber about six miles distant, while on the right and left was timber five to six miles away. It was not the place that Fannin would have selected to make his stand, but he had to play the cards that had been dealt. It was the breakdown of a cart that aborted Fannin's movement to relieve the men in the Alamo, and, now another breakdown of a cart put his entire army at risk.[43]

Despite the confusion the Texans quickly organized their forces to face the enemy on all sides. On the front were the San Antonio Greys and the Red Rovers; to the rear were Duval's Mustangs, plus detachments from Captain Fraser and others; the left was held by Westover's regulars; and on the right was the Mobile Greys. The artillery was located on the corners commanded by Capts. Moore, Holland, Hurst, Schrusnecki, and Petrewich. Those without a unit protected the stranded hospital wagon and used their skill as sharpshooters.[44] In fact, these sharp-shooting frontiersmen caught everyone's attention when they silenced four Carise Indians who had crept in close on a slight rise and were being extremely effective in dropping Texans. Captain Duval was requested to silence these Indians. He took a position near a gun carriage with a clear view of the Indian vantage spot. Using a heavy Kentucky rifle he proceeded to perforate the Indians' heads one by one as they raised to shoot at the embattled Texans. On his last shot one of the fingers on his right hand was taken off by a musket ball.[45]

Harry (Henry D.) Ripley, the nineteen-year-old son of General Ripley of Louisiana, suffered a broken thigh as a result of the Indian sniper fire. It must have made him mad because he induced Mrs. Cash (a non-combatant who had followed her husband) to prop him up in her cart where he had a clear view of the battle. He brought down four Mexicans before a round ball broke his right arm. He addressed Mrs. Cash: "You may take me down now, mother: I have done my share; they have paid exactly two for one on account of both balls in me."[46]

Duval, a soldier who later escaped the massacre, described the action graphically:

> When the Mesicans had approached to within half a mile of our lines they formed into three columns, one remaining stationary, the other two moving to our right and left, but still keeping at about the same distance from us. While they were carrying out this maneuver, our artillery opened upon them with some effect, for now and then we could see a round shot plough through their dense ranks. When the two moving columns, the one on the right and the one on the left, were opposite to each other, they suddenly changed front and the three columns, with trumpets braying and pennons flying, charged upon us simultaneously from three directions. When within three or four hundred yards of our lines our artillery opened upon them with grape and canister shot, with deadly effect, but still their advance was unchecked, until their foremost ranks were in actual contact in some places with the bayonets of our men. But the fire at close quarters from our muskets and rifles was so rapid and destructive, that before long they fell back in confusion, leaving the ground covered in places with horses and dead men.[47]

Horton's Cavalry

What happened to Colonel Horton's cavalry squadron?

Horton's group of thirty-one had been augmented by men from the San Antonio Greys, Red Rovers, and others, increasing the strength to forty. When the Mexicans were contacted most of Horton's men were sent in front to scout out the timber on Coleto Creek. When the Mexican advance guard appeared from a belt of timber on the right, Fannin instructed Captain Holland and Captain Hurst to fall back with their artillery to the rear to engage the Mexicans with a rear guard action, thereby clearing the way for his army to reach the timber in front before stopping. Fannin also expected Horton, on hearing the firing, to return to the Texan lines. Actually, after Fannin's army was formed to make its stand, the cavalry did return and several members of the San Antonio Greys, who were riding with Horton, did break through the Mexican lines and rejoin their unit. Horton's main body left the scene. Historians through the years have debated the issue, but failed to either censure, or approve, Horton's tactics.

Later, Horton himself had this to say about the controversy:

> But what fright took possession of us as we concluded the results of the fateful morning from the position of the Mexican troops! We stood in astonishment and were undecided as what to do, when suddenly the warlike bugle notes of the Mexican cavalry sounded. No time was to be lost; quickly we had to counsel and just as quickly we were ready. If Fannin had so far forgotten his duty to surrender, we were obligated to save ourselves for the republic. Now was the time when Texas needed our arms and our guns. All of our volunteers were now either taken prisoners or were murdered. Consequently we turned our horses and speedily galloped back to Victoria to unite with Houston's troops at Gonzales.

When the Republic was formed, Horton was elected to the first senate.[48]

Sunset brought an end to the shooting as the Mexicans withdrew a respectful distance and set up their campfires and scouting patrols, replete with music and bugle calls that jarred the night. A check showed that only seven Texans had been killed and sixty wounded, forty seriously. The wounded suffered severely during the night due to the lack of water. Without lights, Dr. Barnard was not able to attend to them. Sometime before midnight the word went out for all able-bodied men to dig trenches in the center of the hollow square. Wagons, carts, and dead animals were used to serve as bulwarks. The Mexicans did not reveal the number of killed or wounded; however, Dr. Barnard recalled treating over one hundred men with near fatal wounds and being told that the Mexicans suffered 400 killed on the battle field.[49]

The plight of the wounded touched Mrs. Cash to the extent that at first light she, accompanied by her fourteen-year-old son, went to General Urrea's tent to ask for water for the wounded. Urrea did not reply to her request; his eyes were riveted on her son's shot pouch and powder horn that he had neglected to leave behind. The general lectured: "Woman! Are you not ashamed to bring one of such tender age into such a situation?"

The boy immediately answered him that: "young as he was, he

knew his right, as did everybody in Texas; and he intended to have them or die."

At this crucial point the meeting was interrupted by a white flag raised by the Texans.

Fannin's men had surveyed their plight in the light of a chilly, damp, March morning. Mexican reinforcements had arrived during the night, but of greater importance was the state of their wounded men who badly needed water. The odds were insurmountable— they decided to surrender, if an honorable capitulation could be negotiated.[50]

Capitulation

The matter of capitulation had been thoroughly discussed among the officers, who in turn shared it with their men. When the matter was broached to Colonel Fannin, his first reaction was: "We whipped them off yesterday, and we can do so again today."[51] In the end it was generally agreed that capitulation was the best for the entire command, especially the wounded. Eventually Fannin met with Urrea under a white flag to work out the details. Dr. Joseph E. Field, one of the doctors in Fannin's command, was quoted as saying: "When the two commanders met at a proper distance from their respective armies, the Mexican General embraced Colonel Fannin and said, 'Yesterday we fought; but today we are friends.'" Capitulation terms were agreed upon and written in English and Spanish. Fannin was joined in the surrender talks by Maj. Benjamin C. Wallace, second in command, and Capt. Durangue, an interpreter. The four principal points were as follows:

1. That we should be received and treated as prisoners of war according to the usage of the most civilized nations.
2. That private property should be respected and restored: The side arms of officers should be given up.
3. That the men should be sent to Copano, and thence to the United States in eight days, or as soon thereafter as vessels could be procured to take them.
4. That the officers should be paroled and returned to the United States in like manner.[52]

In contrast to the above articles, Urrea declared that the following terms were signed by Fannin. As you can see they are somewhat different:

1. The Mexican troops, having planted their artillery at the distance of one hundred and seventy paces, and having opened their fire, we raised the white flag, and instantly there came Colonels Morales and Holsinger, and to them we proposed surrender at discretion, on terms they should judge suitable.
2. That the wounded, and that the commander, Fannin, be treated with all possible consideration, it being proposed that we should lay down our arms.
3. That all the detachment shall be treated as prisoners-of-war and placed at the disposal of the supreme government.

> Dated: March 20th, 1836
> B. C. Wallace, Major
> J. M. Chadwick,
> Approved: J. W. Fannin,
> Commander

General Urrea later made the following three entries in his diary:

When the enemy raised the white flag I sent to inform their leader that I could admit of no other terms than those of surrendering at discretion without any modification whatsoever. . . .

If you are willing to surrender at discretion, the thing is concluded; if otherwise, I will return to my post, and the attack shall continue. . . .

Fannin was a respectable man, and a man of courage, a quality reciprocally prized by soldiers in the field. His manners conciliated my esteem, and had it been in my power to save him, as well as his companions, I should have felt gratified in so doing. All the assurance I could make him was, that I would interpose in his behalf with the general-in-chief, which I did, in a letter from Victoria.

To these entries Urrea claims to have received an answer from Santa Anna dated Bexar, March 23, 1836, from which he gives the following extract: "In respect to the prisoners of whom you speak in your last communication, you must not fail to bear in mind the circular of the supreme government, in which it is decreed, that foreigners invading the republic, and taken with arms in their hands, shall be judged and treated as pirates."[53]

All of the surrender terms were accomplished on Sunday, March 20. As soon as the word was official, Dr. Barnard; Dr. J. E. Field; Dr. John Shackelford (Shackelford was captain of the Red Rovers that he had recruited and equipped in Alabama and brought to Texas); and Dr. Ferguson, a student of Dr. Shackleford, attended to the wounded. Dr. Shackelford, who was among those spared at the massacre, recalled the first words of Colonel Holsinger, a German engineer in the Mexican service, when he entered the American lines: "Well, gentlemen, in eight days, liberty and home!" Dr. Barnard, who was also spared, confirmed these words.[54]

As soon as the battlefield formalities were ended all able-bodied men were posted off to Goliad under a strong guard. The wounded were left behind until carts could be procured to move them. They reached the old fort at sunset and were literally driven into the chapel where they were forced to keep the center space open for the guards to pass, under the threat of the discharge of guns. The doctors started dressing wounds at first light only to be summoned by Mexican officers to dress wounds of the Mexican soldiers.[55]

The days following the Battle of Coleto brought little cheer to the prisoners. Mexican guards systematically helped themselves to personal items like blankets, watches, clothing, and anything else that they fancied. Dr. Barnard's surgical instruments were stolen and Colonel Fannin demanded that they be returned under terms of the capitulation as private property, to no avail. The week dragged on with few bright notes. One did come when Colonel Fannin, accompanied by Colonel Holsinger, went to Copano to arrange for transportation for the Texans to go to New Orleans. The ship they were seeking had already sailed. Did Colonel Holsinger know this, or was he not privy to what was going on in the high command? On March 23 Major Miller and his Tennessee volunteers were brought in to the fort. They had been captured when their ship landed at Copano. On March 25 what was left of Colonel Ward's command was brought in from Victoria. Other prisoners were brought in as they were captured.[56]

The night of March 26 was not much different from others except that a sense of well-being had settled over the men. Colonel

Fannin had returned that day from Port Copano where he was seeking a ship to take the troops to New Orleans. This thought cheered the men. The trip was made at the suggestion of the Mexican command. Fannin and several of the doctors chatted about the prospects of reaching the United States. Music from a flute drifted from where the men bedded down. Strains of *Home, Sweet Home* drifted through the air.[57]

Little did these men know that at 7 P.M. that night a rider from Bexar arrived with a message from General Santa Anna addressed to Colonel Nicholas de la Portilla, commandant of the Goliad forces. The message read:

> I am informed that there have been sent to you by General Urrea two hundred and thirty-four prisoners, taken in the action of Encinal de Perdido on the 19th and 20th of the present month; and, as the supreme government has ordered that all foreigners taken with arms in their hands, making war upon the nation, shall be treated as pirates, I have been surprised that the circular of the said supreme government has not been fully compiled with in this particular; I therefore order that you should give immediate effect to the said ordinance in respect to all those foreigners, who have yielded to the force of arms, having had the audacity to come and insult the Republic, to devastate with fire and sword, as has been the case in Goliad, causing vast detriment to our citizens; in a word shedding the precious blood of Mexican citizens, whose only crime has been fidelity to their country. I trust that, in reply to this, you will inform me that public vengeance has been satisfied, by the punishment of such detestable delinquents. I transcribe the said decree for your guidance, and, that you may strictly fulfill the same, in the zealous hope, that, for the future, the provisions of the supreme government may not for a moment be infringed. (signed) Antonio Lopez de Santa Anna, Headquarters, Bexar.[58]

March 27—Palm Sunday Massacre

Presumably Colonel Portilla met with his staff immediately after receiving General Santa Anna's death decree in order to plan the operation. It was obvious that the entire execution was carried out in minute detail with every player in the drama fully briefed. Portilla put the plan into operation at daybreak with each staff member carrying out his designated role. Capt. (Dr.) Jack Shackelford told how his part worked: "At dawn of day we were awakened by a Mexican officer calling up, and saying he wanted the men to form a line, that they might be counted.... After leaving the church, I was met by Colonel Guerrera, said to be the Adjutant General of the Mexican army.... He requested that I would go to his tent, in company with Major Miller and men; and that I would take my friend and companion, Dr. Joseph H. Barnard, with me."[59] These men were among the ones spared from the massacre.

Survivors of the death march told of having no misgivings when they were awakened and told to muster with full gear. Stories of Santa Anna arriving to pardon them, or of going to Port Copano were passed from man to man. Capt. Benjamin Holland, a survivor, told the story of how the prisoners were divided into three groups and marched off on three different roads:

> The Mexicans had always said that Santa Anna would be at La Bahia on the 27th to release us. Accordingly on that day, we were ordered to form all the prisoners; we were told that we were going to bring wood and water, and that Santa Anna would be there that day; we were ordered to march all the officers at the head of the file.... As we marched out of the sally port we saw hollow squares formed ready to receive us; we were ordered to file left, and marched into a hollow square of double filed cavalry, on foot, armed with carbines, and broad swords.
>
> This square was filled and closed, and the head of the remaining files wheeled off into the other squares, and so on, until all were strongly guarded in squares; the company of which this writer was one, was ordered to forward and no more was seen of our unfortunate comrades; we were marched out in the Bexar Road, near the burying ground, and as we were ordered to halt we heard our companions shrieking in the most agonizing tones, Oh, God! Oh, God! Spare us! and nearly simultaneously a report of musketry. It was then we knew what was to be our fate. The writer of this then observed to Major Wallace he best to make a desperate rush—he said, "No," we were too strongly guarded—he then sprung and struck a soldier on his right a severe blow with his fist, they being at open files, the soldier at the outer file

attempting to shoot him, but too close was unable, the soldier then turned his gun and struck the writer a severe blow upon the left hand. I then seized hold of the gun and wrenched it from his hand and instantly started and ran toward the river.... Holland and twenty-seven other men managed to get into the brush, or river, and escape, their harrowing tales found their way into books and newspapers over the years.[60]

John Duval's account was a bit more graphic:

When about a mile above town, a halt was made and the guard on the side next the river filed around to the opposite side. Hardly had this maneuver been executed, when I heard a heavy firing of musketry in the directions taken by the other two divisions. Someone near me exclaimed: "Boys they are going to shoot us!" and at the same instant I heard the clicking of musket locks all along the Mexican line. I turned to look, and as I did so, the Mexicans fired upon us, killing probably one hundred out of the one hundred and fifty men in the division. The man in front of me was shot dead, and in falling he knocked me down. I didn't get up for a minute, and when I rose to my feet, I found that the whole Mexican line had charged over me, and were in hot pursuit.... I followed on after them ... one of the soldiers charged upon me with his bayonet (his gun I suppose being empty). As he lunged at me, one of our men coming from another direction, ran between us, and the bayonet was driven through his body. The blow was given with such force that in falling, the man probably wrenched, or twisted the bayonet in such a way as to prevent the Mexican from withdrawing it immediately. Duval made it to the river where he joined up with John Holliday and Samuel T. Brown.[61]

Second Sgt. Isaac D. Hamilton was a member of the Red Rovers. In the first volley of Mexican musket fire a ball tore through the flesh of his left thigh. In the terror-stricken seconds between the reality of what was happening, and the searing wound, Hamilton's eye had spotted a low spot in a sagging brush fence. He plunged, jumping as high as he could, but while still in the air a bayonet plunged into his right thigh. Blood spurting from his wounds didn't stop his headlong flight through the scene of horror as Mexican soldiers bayoneted and clubbed fleeing Texans. He finally made it into waist-high grass on the prairie and then into a line of timber.

Eventually he joined up with Zachariah Brooks, from his own Alabama hometown and company. Later the two joined up with Wilson Simpson and Dullard Cooper. A great-great nephew of Hamilton told the story in the book *Goliad Survivor*.[62]

The fact that all Mexicans were not as evil as Santa Anna can be seen in the acts of kindness that saved others from the massacre. The "Angel of Goliad," Senora Francisca (Panchita) Alvarez, the beautiful wife of Capt. Telesforo Alvarez, an officer in Col. Don Francisco Garay's command, was credited with hiding several soldiers from death after she found out what was in store for them on Palm Sunday. Earlier, she had interceded on behalf of Colonel Miller's men who were taken captive at Copano Bay. Seeing how the ropes were cutting into the flesh of their wrists, she managed to get her husband to loosen the ropes.[63] All of Miller's men were saved from the massacre because "they had entered Texas unarmed." Actually, they had shucked their uniforms when their ship anchored and gone for a swim, wading ashore naked, at which time they were captured. Another story was that when confronted by armed soldiers they threw their guns and ammunition overboard and swore they were unarmed.

Colonel Garay also went to where Drs. Barnard, Shackelford, and Field were sleeping and removed them to a safe room where they remained during the massacre (no mention is made of Dr. Furgeson). He also sought out a young San Patricio soldier, Andrew O'Boyle, and saved him from the slaughter. Several weeks before, he had dined at the home of an Irish woman (Mary O'Boyle) in San Patricio who asked him that if he encountered her brother, Andrew O'Boyle, to be "kind" to him.

The story of William L. Hunter, a lawyer who joined the New Orleans Greys, exemplifies the fact that kindness can overcome. This young soldier was felled by a ball in the massacre volley. As he lay stunned, a soldier cut his throat, and then to make sure he was dead he thrust him with his bayonet and clubbed him with the butt of his gun before stripping him of his clothes. When nightfall came the wounded soldier struggled to the river, crossed over, and made his way to Manahuilla Creek and finally wandered into a Mexican ranch. A woman found and concealed him. Each night she brought food and water until he was able to travel, and dressed him in clothing she "liberated" from her men folk.[64]

Following the shooting of the unarmed prisoners in Fannin's command, the Mexican troops returned to the presidio to finish their grisly job by shooting the wounded. Andrew M. O'Boyle told the story best:

> A Mexican officer came into the hospital, and ordered me to tell all those able to walk to go outside ... those too severely wounded to walk were carried out by soldiers ... a file of men under a corporal took two of our number, marched them out toward the company, and after bandaging their eyes made them lie with their faces to the ground, after which, placing the muzzles close to their heads, shot them as they lay ... an officer, apparently of distinction, came into the yard and asked in a loud voice, in English, whether anyone named O'Boyle was there or not. I was near him and answered at once.

O'Boyle's life was spared because his sister and brother in San Patricio were polite to General Garay when he spent the night in their home several weeks before when the Mexican army moved through the old city.[65]

Fannin was the last to die. He was brought out of the hospital and informed of his imminent execution. He asked that he be shot in the breast and not in the head and handed his watch to the man in charge with the request that he be decently interred. Fannin was shot in the head and the soldier pocketed the watch. His stripped body was dumped with the rest. Later, the corpses were placed in several large piles. Brush was stacked on them to form a funeral pyre and burned.[66] Much has been written about General Santa Anna flashing the secret Mason sign at San Jacinto. Evidently the fact that Fannin was a Mason did not save him even though several of the Mexican officers were Masons.[67]

The massacre at Goliad, preceded by the fall of the Alamo on March 6, galvanized attention in the United States, and to a lesser extent in Europe, toward the Texas Revolution. The revulsion at shooting down unarmed men who had surrendered was shocking to such an extent that indignation poured out of the United States in the form of men and arms to assist in the battle against the tyrant— Santa Anna. The Napoleon of the West surely would have profited more by sending Fannin's men back to New Orleans in utter defeat so that the world could see them in their darkest hour. Instead, these volunteers, most of them from the United States, were held on high as martyrs who died at the hand of a despot who was a foe to democracy.

Goliad, which had been the center of attention before and after the fall of the Alamo, quickly slid out of the forefront in the battle for Texas Independence. The spotlight turned to Gen. Sam Houston. Houston, after retiring from the scene in disgust with the muddling of the army's top command, returned from the Indian Nation in time for the Texas Declaration of Independence Convention on March 2, 1836. On March 4 Houston was named major general, and commander in chief of the land forces of the Texian army—regulars, volunteers, and militia. This ended the duplicity of command. By March 11 he was issuing orders from Gonzales where he had gone to assess firsthand how to cope with Santa Anna. He reported finding "Upwards of three hundred men in camp, without organization." This number increased to 400 by March 13.[68]

7.

FALL OF THE ALAMO

Lt. Col. James C. Neill, an old veteran of the Indian wars in the United States, was appointed commander of the San Antonio force when the veterans of the Battle of Bexar pulled out.[1] Later Gen. Sam Houston put James Bowie in command. Between the two commanders they had about 110 men. Actually, Bowie had been sent to the Alamo to blow it up, but like all frontier commanders, Bowie and Neill didn't approve of the idea and the Alamo was not destroyed.[2] On February 3, 1836, Col. William Barret Travis brought another thirty men into the compound. Col. Davy Crockett rode into town on February 8 at the head of twelve men who called themselves the Tennessee Company of Mounted Volunteers.

On February 23, after the Mexican armies again threatened San Antonio, Colonel Travis put out a plea for men to join in the defense of the Alamo.[3] Thirty-two men from Gonzales broke through Santa Anna's lines on March 1 and joined the beleaguered Alamo defenders.[4] Colonel Travis issued his famous appeal to "Fellow Citizens and Compatriots," closing it with "Victory or Death."[5] Bonham rode to Goliad seeking aid for the second time from Colonel Fannin, but returned on March 3 emptyhanded. For three more days the valiant band of patriots, frontiersmen, statesmen, and plain men held the Mexicans at bay only to be put to the sword on March 6 as Mexican soldiers broke through the walls. The hand-to-hand fighting was fierce but finally silence fell over the scene. Santa Anna was reported to have said that, "it was but a small affair." Never has one man so underestimated the outrage that comes from a valiant defense.[6]

Still another version of the fall of the Alamo comes from Jose Enrique de la Pena, an officer on Santa Anna's staff. His version tells that Crockett and six other defenders were taken alive and brought to Santa Anna, who ordered them shot.[7]

News of the siege of the Alamo spread quickly through the nearby settlements. Once again men put aside their plows and headed for Gonzales.

Texas' Lexington Threatened Once Again

Convention Hall, San Felipe, March 2, 1836

Almost before the smoke from the fall of the Alamo on March 6 had cleared away, volunteers from the surrounding communities began to come into Gonzles at a steady pace. The mood was bullish as the volunteers pushed to whip the Mexicans and get home in time to milk the cows. A large corn field belonging to Eli Mitchell was picked as a camp site for the volunteers to accommodate the number that had grown to over three hundred.[8] Sam Houston described the situation:

> War is raging on the frontiers . . . It is rumored that the enemy are on their march to Gonzales, and that they have entered the colonies. The fate of Bexar is unknown. The country must and shall be defended. The patriots of Texas are appealed to in behalf of their bleeding.
> (Signed) Sam Houston, Commander-in-Chief of the Army.[9]

When General Houston issued this assessment on March 2, 1836, he was in attendance at Convention Hall, San Felipe, for the signing of the declaration of independence. Later the General Council named him commander in chief of the Texas army. Tragically, the men who had challenged Houston for the top post of commander, namely, James Walker Fannin, Frank Johnson, and

James Grant, had ceased to be contenders. Johnson survived the Battle of San Patricio, but never sought a leadership role again. Colonel Fannin was a Mexican prisoner and was facing his end at Goliad. Captain Grant was killed in a Mexican ambush on March 2. This finally gave Houston, and only Houston, complete charge of the Texas armed effort. He spent the next few days making plans on how to stop General Santa Anna, who had headed his army east after putting the Alamo to the sword on March 6.

General Houston evidently knew that the Alamo had fallen by at least March 11 when he arrived in Gonzales to take charge of forces gathering in that city.[10] On the same day Houston issued orders to Colonel Fannin to blow up the fortress in Goliad and fall back to Victoria. Fannin elected to disobey, and "held a council of war, and that he had determined to defend the place, and called it Fort Defiance, and had taken the responsibility to disobey the order." On the following day General Houston addressed a letter to Philip Dimmitt directing him to bring his command, as well as any troops not needed in Victoria, and report to Gonzales.[11] While he was still in San Felipe he dispatched *empresario* Sterling Robertson to the United States to raise troops for service in Texas.[12] Over the next several weeks more and more volunteers joined the army.

Houston Takes Command of the Army at Gonzales

At dusk on the day of Houston's arrival in Gonzales (March 11), Anselmo Bogarra and another Mexican arrived with news about the fall of the Alamo. Houston, seeking to prevent panic, put the two Mexicans under arrest as spies and sent Deaf Smith, Henry Karnes, and R. E. Handy toward Bexar to check the situation. They met Mrs. Almeron (Susan) Dickinson with her infant daughter and two servants who reported that the Alamo had been put to the sword and her husband, Lieutenant Dickinson, a Gonzales resident, was killed. In all, thirty-one men from Gonzales lost their lives in the Alamo. Karnes hastened back to Houston with the confirmation while others escorted Mrs. Dickinson to Gonzales.[13]

One of Houston's first orders was to organize the approximately 400 men who were gathered in Gonzales. The volunteers were mainly Texans from the Brazos, Colorado, and Guadalupe river valleys, plus the Kentucky volunteers, under the command of Capt. Sidney Sherman. The make-up of this army, and that commanded by Colonel Fannin, was different in that Fannin's men came directly from the United States. Edwin Burleson was elected colonel; Sidney Sherman, lieutenant colonel; and Alexander Somerville, major of the regiment. The group took the name of the First Regiment of the Volunteer Army of Texas.

Houston spent only a short time pondering his course of action. He ordered camp broken and the First Regiment was in retreat, getting started at 11 P.M. on March 13. In fact, the action was taken with such haste that no one recalled the picket guard on the road leading to Bexar. Captain Sharp, one of the pickets, remembered Colonel Handy and Captain Karnes coming back to alert them. Three cannons, including the two brass twenty-four-pound cannons, were thrown into the river to prevent them from falling into the hands of the Mexicans. As the troops readied to leave, Houston issued an order to burn the town of Gonzales to the ground to prevent it, too, from falling into the hands of the enemy.

Captain Sharp remembered the fateful night: "We divided ourselves into two parties, one party to commence at one end of the town and the other at the other end and meet. There were some four or five in each party, and we made rapid work of it. The houses were principally framed, covered with thin boards split from the oak, similar to barrel staves. In the course of a few minutes the flames began their work of destruction and by dawn every house was burning, or had crumpled to ashes." There were thirty homes in Gonzales on this date and when the fires were out only two small structures were left standing on March 14, 1836—Adam Zumwalt's kitchen and Andrew Ponton's smokehouse. Both had been overlooked.[14]

Hysteria ran rampant as the troops started their retreat. Men were bidding farewell to their families as they rode off with Houston's army. The women, now in charge of the household, were left with an empty feeling as they prepared to flee ahead of General Santa Anna's army. The Runaway Scrape[15] was underway as women, children and old men loaded what belongings they could carry onto carts and wagons and buried the rest and headed east. Fear was mirrored in every eye. It would be about six agonizing weeks before peace would return to the Guadalupe valley and homes would be rebuilt in Gonzales. Jeff Parsons, a slave belonging to Maj. George Sutherland of Jackson County, gave a graphic account that ran in the *Galveston News*:

> The women, children, slaves, and a few old men reached the Sabine before the Battle of San Jacinto. There was a lot of scared folks in the runaway crowd. Some went on sleds, some on contrivances made with truck wheels, some on wagons, some on horseback, some on foot, or any way they could get there. . . . the children were crying, the women praying and the old men cursing. . . .[16]

Victory at San Jacinto

Houston continued his retreat, and, as troops and critics carped, he kept his counsel and doggedly stayed on the run. He finally seized the right moment to attack on April 21, 1836, when Santa Anna's army was enjoying *siesta* time on the banks of the San Jacinto River. The blood curdling yells of "Remember the Alamo" and "Remember Goliad" put fear into the hearts of Mexican soldiers and brought an uneasy peace to Texas. A new Republic was born.[17] However, it was to remain the Raw Frontier for many long, painful years.

8.

CATTLE DRIVES IN THE RAW FRONTIER

The cattle industry in the Raw Frontier struggled from the very beginning. In the early days Indians were the biggest problem, but before long the white cattle rustlers were the feared adversaries. But despite all of the problems, the cattle industry grew, and in fact it was the major source of income for Texas in its early days.

The cattle that the settlers found in Texas when they arrived in the 1820s were descendants of the cattle that Christopher Columbus brought to the New World on his second voyage in 1493. He introduced not only cattle, but horses, hogs, and sheep to Hispanola, or Santo Domingo. Three of Columbus's voyages carried cattle. In 1503 Queen Isabella of Spain ordered all ships headed for the Indies to carry livestock. Eventually the newly introduced animals found their way to the mainland.[1]

By 1778 Espiritu Santo Mission[2] estimated that at branding time they had over 15,000 head of cattle that belonged to the mission. No one knows how many other cattle roamed over southern Texas. About the only use the mission had for cattle was meat for their Indian residents and for barter with other missions in East Texas and Louisiana. Little money changed hands on these deals— trade goods such as corn and other supplies were used for payment.

Large amounts of cattle were slaughtered by soldiers and

settlers for their hides and tallow. Spanish kings at various times sought to turn the stocks of cattle into cash for the crown but none were successful.[3]

Don Felix DeLeon, son of *empresario* Don Martin DeLeon, made a good living before the Texas Revolution supplying horses, mules, and cattle to the New Orleans market.[4]

A census in Texas in 1783 showed that there were 2,819 Spanish subjects in the province of Texas, the vast majority being ranchers who had followed the missionaries into Texas and settled around La Bahia at Goliad, Bexar, and in East Texas, and who had secured grants of land to carry on ranching.

Ranching in South Texas might have been a bit different if it had not been for Marques de Rubi, who was commissioned by the king of Spain in 1766 to make an inventory of the Spanish presence in Texas. Rubi disagreed with the Spanish who were considering that perhaps some, or all of it should be abandoned. As for the Gulf Coast, he advised that "the presidio of Bahia del Espiritu Santo should remain where it was, on the San Antonio River . . . to protect the well-stocked ranches already established . . ."[5]

"The Round-up—On Paloduro Ranch, Paloduro, Texas."
—Photo courtesy Institute of Texan Cultures.

Historian Walter Prescott Webb described the cattle kingdom of Texas like a diamond—the four points being San Antonio to Brownsville and Old Indianola to Laredo.[6] The great cattle trails that led to the north and west reached into this cattle basin.

Before the big drives got under way there were lots of smaller efforts to get cattle to market. In 1779 about 2,000 head of cattle were driven to New Orleans, consigned to feed the army of Bernardo de Galvez. He had been commissioned by the King of Spain to engage the British on the Gulf of Mexico, in order to lend assistance to the Americans who were struggling to gain their independence from England. In a short time over 9,000 head of Texas cattle went to New Orleans for this purpose.[7] Cattle headed from Texas to New Orleans, even after the great trails were opened to Abilene, Kansas, and other rail heads. The old crossing on the Sabine River at Niblett's Bluff flourished in the late 1850s and into the 1860s, probably getting beef to the Confederate forces. In 1912 a Mrs. William Dunn, who had lived at Niblett's Bluff, wrote a letter to the *Houston Post* (picked up later by the *Beaumont Journal*) telling the story of wagon trains and herds of cattle moving over the road at Niblett's Bluff headed for New Orleans. Special areas were set up for the wagons and stock where they could be cared for while drivers and cowboys refreshed themselves at the town's two hotels, the Hartman and the Trunbull.[8]

Not only were cattle abundant in the Raw Frontier, there were huge herds of mustangs that inhabited the area. One favorite method of penning these wild horses was to capture one and tie a straw man on his back and turn him loose to rejoin the herd. The horses would spook at the straw man and would run en masse, making a rolling, roaring noise as they crashed through the brush. After the horses had exhausted themselves, the cowboys would enter and herd them toward a pen with wide wings. Once they were inside, the gates were closed. Many ranchers got their start with horses in this manner.[9]

In an effort to tap the vast cattle resources in the Raw Frontier Gen. Felix Huston, commanding officer of the army of the Republic who was inclined to be an adventurer, offered to lead an expedition into the area between the San Antonio and Nueces rivers to round up stock for the army's use, with the volunteers get-

Engraving of cowboys on the trail with cattle, sketched by Warren Johnson.
—Photo courtesy Institute of Texan Cultures.

ting an interest in the venture. John Linn had been advocating any plan that would keep the stock out of the hands of enemies.[10]

The cattle problem did not go away with statehood. Late in December of 1848 Maj. J. M. La Motte, a commander of U.S. forces in Texas, sent a letter to the *alcalde* in Camargo, Mexico, which called attention to the fact that Mexicans were crossing the border and driving cattle and horses back to Mexico. La Motte promised due process of law for those caught. *Alcalde* J. Maria G. Villarreal answered tartly that, "Mexicans have held property in Texas from time immemorial. . . ." He also pointed out that the treaty that ended the war guaranteed Mexicans rights to their property.[11]

Some of the earliest cattle drives out of San Patricio County were organized and run by Marcellus and George Turner, with Marcellus doing most of the work. The Turners went into the cattle business during the days of the open range, filing on a piece of land[12] near where Chiltipin Creek runs into the Arkansas River. In 1858 Marcellus and T. M. Coleman put together a herd and started them up the trail. Letters written by Marcellus gave an almost day-to-day account of the drive.[13] They crossed the Red River at Preston and by May 5 they were within two days of the Aransas River. At this point Marcellus left the drive and rode into Leavenworth, Kansas, and sold out to army contractors. By mid-June he had cashed the government drafts in St. Louis and was on the way home.

In the winter of 1858 Marcellus Turner, Jonathan Newman, and Tom Coleman formed the Star Company. They coordinated drives in three herds. Marcellus left with 630 head. Newman followed with 650 head and Coleman left the Chiltipin Ranch with 1,100 head. They were able to sell the first two herds, but found no market for the third. They went to Chicago with the last herd and finally butchered the cattle and shipped the pickled hams to New York. The Star Company was getting by but not getting rich.[14]

An unwritten law prevailed in the Raw Frontier, which said that if a rancher caught a man putting a hot iron on one of his cows he could kill him. The grand jury would indict the crime, but each time the case came to trial it would be passed until it was finally transferred to an adjoining county where it was finally dropped. Marcellus Turner, Tom Coleman, H. H. Hunter, and Wiley Hodges evidently thought they had justification when two squatters moved onto their open range and settled. The ranchers sent word for the men to leave, but they answered: "We are going to homestead—get your cattle out of our way!" The ranchers did a bit of checking and found that one of the men, Martin, had been butchering their cattle, so they armed themselves and presented their search warrant (cocked rifles) and found hides with their brand in his possession. They tied him up and traveled a short distance to where another squatter, Carter, lived. They left Martin tied to a tree while they rode up to Carter's house. They called him out and told him to move. He said "no way" and turned to walk back into his shack when a rifle bullet caught him in the back. As they rode away somehow or other Martin was left swinging in a tree. On schedule an indictment was handed down and the case was passed twice before being sent to Goliad County where it was eventually dropped. The cattlemen were still kings of the open range.[15]

Beef impressment[16] by Confederate forces hit hard in Live Oak County in late 1864 when Gen. John Magruder ordered the taking of beef without payment. The editor of a Corpus Christi newspaper probably reflected the sentiment of ranchers when he wrote: ". . . those whose beeves may be taken by the press-gang on this river (Nueces) . . . to proceed against them as if they were common depredators and test their papers and authority in a court of law."[17]

Something about Oakville seemed to attract cattle thieves. A couple of years earlier a Mexican and a man by the name of Dinah, plus two vaqueros, showed up in Oakville with some forty head of cattle headed for the Rio Grande. After they left town the sheriff decided to do a bit of investigating. He rode out and caught up with the herd, which had increased to 140 including a number of Live Oak brands. The vaqueros took off and the cattle and the two owners returned to Oakville. The editor closed with: "Further deponent saith not."[18] He probably knew that Oakville justice had been swift and sure.

Cattlemen's concerns in Nueces, San Patricio, and Live Oak counties were underlined by an ad in the *Nueces Valley* on August 7, 1858, when seven leading stockmen in the area called a meeting for Wednesday, August 18, 1858 at 11 A.M. for the purpose of organizing a "Stock Association." More newspapers in this period are missing, but oral tradition tells that R. D. Love, one of the signers, went on to organize a militant group designed to cut down on cattle rustling.

The Civil War and Reconstruction had a chilling effect on the cattle market. In fact, there was virtually no market. The price of cattle dropped so low that trailing and shipping were too expensive. Cattle were worthless except for their tallow, bones, and hides. This gave rise to a unique marketing device—the packeries that slaughtered cattle, saved the hide,[19] tallow, and bones and dumped the meat in huge, stinking piles. Packeries sprang up mainly along the coast where cattle were shipped. Rockport was probably one of the best examples of the packery phenomenon. Conceived as a port city to ship cattle, it became a packery city in a short time when market prices fell too low to ship cattle profitably. Within a matter of months as many as a dozen large concerns were in the business. A large packery, employing forty men, could process 200 to 250 head of cattle per day. Cushman and Company was the largest in Rockport and was capable of slaughtering up to 5,000 animals yearly.

An ugly chapter in history was written during this period. A maverick, an unbranded calf, was considered fair game to anyone, and, likewise, a person who found a dead animal on the open range was allowed to skin the animal and claim the hide as his own, regardless of whose brand it might be wearing. This led rustlers to slaughter animals and take their hides, claiming that they found the cattle dead. Ranchers took desperate measures to protect their cattle. Ranchers and skinners were killed in the so-called "Skinning War."[20]

Shanghai Pierce, a rough and ready cattleman from the upper coast area, organized a posse to search out and punish thieves working in the area. The posse saw smoke coming out of a brush area close to Palacios Creek. Circling until they found a trail, the cattlemen found hides spread out to dry on bushes bearing brands from all over the area. A clearing produced a woman, children, and several men. Another trail led to the creek where a schooner was anchored to take on hides and tallow. Frontier justice was swift, but I. N. Mitchell, a respected rancher, protested the hanging of a married man. Pierce agreed and a Mr. Lunn, his wife, and children were loaded into a wagon and instructed to not come back into the county again. The Matagorda grand jury indicted W. W. Lunn for stealing cattle hides. As to the hangings, the sheriff put Able Head "Shanghai" Pierce under bond to appear as a state witness. Shanghai, probably sensing that hanging was frowned upon, converted cattle into gold and spent eighteen months in Kansas.[21]

Shanghai Pierce was a legend in South Texas, especially in the sweep from Matagorda, Jackson, Victoria, Goliad, and Lavaca counties. He came to Texas from New York. As a raw-boned youth of nineteen he stowed away on a boat bound for Indianola, and upon his discovery he worked out a deal for his passage in exchange for work. He landed in Indianola and soon struck a deal with Richard "Bing" Grimes to split rails. Pierce asked that his wages be paid in cattle at the end of a year—he wanted to be a cattleman. Trials and tribulations were many, but Shanghai Pierce rode his way to become one of the largest ranchers in the area and a mover of men and cattle. Together with his brother, Jonathan, and Allen and Poole, they ran more than 100,000 head of cattle on the Rancho Grande that was located on Tres Palacios Creek. Not only did he ship cattle by boat to Cuba and New Orleans, he took herds overland to New Orleans, finding a route through the marshes in Louisiana, thereby giving rise to the term "sea lions" applied to his herds of cattle.

Shanghai worked to find something to eradicate cattle ear ticks and is credited, along with Al McFadden and A. P. Borden, in bringing Brahman cattle to the United States. The cattle arrived and the government refused to allow them to enter until Borden interceded with Pres. Theodore Roosevelt.[22]

Waste from the packeries was stacking up near the bay on the north side of the Rockport harbor. A favorite local story told about a Yankee showing up in town inquiring about who owned the mountain of rotted waste. The owner chuckled to himself as he took the proceeds of the sale to the bank. The Yankee disappeared and was almost forgotten until he showed up one day aboard an incoming boat with a load of machinery. He ground up the "hash" and put it in sacks, labeling it *fertilizer*. He made a sizable wad selling the sacked "hash."

During the time that the coastal area ports were being established, cattle was trailed into Indianola, St. Mary's, Rockport, and Corpus Christi, and loaded onto ships that had brought lumber into the area. A lot of these ships were destined for Cuba.[24] Shanghai Pierce was a big player in shipping cattle by boat out of Indianola, especially to Cuba where he established firm sources.[25] Too often writers and historians imagine a giant river of cattle headed up the trail, which did happen, but a large number were sold to packeries and also shipped out of the area ports. The *Corpus Christi Gazette* recognized this market: "The packeries at home, combined with shipments to New Orleans and Havana, have this past season absorbed the greater portion of our first class cattle. This will necessarily reduce the drive to Kansas in the spring to probably not over 10,000 head from the counties of Nueces, San Patricio and Live Oak . . ."

Old records of the giant[26] Coleman, Mathis, Fulton Cattle Company, with headquarters in Rockport, show well over 100,000 head of cattle shipped out of Rockport. They also trailed some to Indianola, during their first five years of existence.

When St. Mary's of Aransas was at its height in the late 1850s cattle pens were built close to the wharves to hold cattle so that when lumber boats were unloaded the live cattle could be loaded for shipment to New Orleans and Cuba. At the same time the growth of the packeries was evident as large amounts of hides, tallow, and bones were being shipped. Salt that was produced by William Brightman and James R. McCarty out of nearby Mission Lake was used on the hides so that they could be shipped "green." These hides brought a better price than the ones that were dried. Ships did not leave the harbor empty. When they did not have cargo they had to take on ballast in order for the ship to handle with ease. This was especially true if the sailing vessels got into bad weather.[27]

On September 24, 1848, the schooner *Louise Antoinette* sailed from Indian Point with a cargo of 120 beef cattle, six mules, and a herd of frightened deer. In 1849 the steamer *Jerry Smith*, operated by the Morgan Line, took on a load of live cattle from Indian Point. Up to that time shipment of cattle had been in sailing vessels, but since steam vessels could be depended upon for being closer to a set time schedule, they became the favorite mode of moving cattle. Cattle shipments out of Indianola, St. Mary's of Aransas, Rockport, and Corpus Christi filled a need to get cattle to the more populated areas in the East. After the Civil War in 1865 cattle shipments out of Indianola amounted to 12,056.[28] While shipment by boat did furnish a bit of relief for the ranchers it could not come close to overland drives in numbers, where an average drive could easily be as much as the yearly total by boat.

Another South Texas rancher who sent a number of herds up the trail in the 1870s was D. C. Rachal. E. R. "Nute" Rachal, brother of D. C. Rachal, was the trail boss on one herd of 1,200 cattle, which included some from the T. M. Coleman ranch on the Chiltipin Creek, for which they paid ten dollars per head. The herd started up the trail about March 20, 1871. They faced all types of hardships, including a herd of bison that caused a stampede and a thunderstorm that mixed the Rachal herd with the Gravis herd. After all of their problems they found a soft market. The entire trip took eight months.[29]

Big cattle drives were put together by men in Nueces County and combined with the massive herds of Capt. Richard King and Capt. Mifflin Kenedy. They amounted to a vast movement of cattle to the rail heads. The *Corpus Christi Gazette* reported on February 22, 1876, that King had sent Capt. Thomas Beynon to Corpus Christi to outfit ninety drovers that were headed up the trail with 17,500 head of cattle. Drives of this size were usually broken down into several herds. Most of the cattle drives that developed in Kleberg and Nueces counties swung to the west before crossing the Nueces River and went northwest through Live Oak, McMullen, La Salle, Dimmitt, Zavala, Uvalde, and Edwards counties and intersected the

Western trail. It then turned north crossing the Red River at Doan's Store. This route was known as the southern route of the Western Trail.[30] Probably one of the biggest years was 1871 when it was estimated that more than 700,000 cattle went up the trails into Kansas and Nebraska.[31] This glut of cattle on the market forced herds to be held over on the northern pastures and in the following winter over 250,000 cattle froze to death on the midwest plains.[32]

Branch Isbell, a footloose cowboy, worked his way into South Texas and worked for several outfits, including Jim Miller of Banquete, Nueces County. Like all cowhands, if there was a dance, he showed up, which was the case in San Patricio where he encountered Lizzie Hinnant. He asked for a dance, and to his embarrassment she gave him a curt, "NO." Seeking to even the score he shot back, "there are other fish in the sea, I'll cast my line in another place." With the same "go to hell" look, Liz replied, "sure, but they are tired of biting at toads." And that was the end of the flirtation. In 1877 he threw in with G. W. Waddell and trailed a herd of stock cattle to Mitchell County in West Texas.[33]

One drive out of Nueces County broke with tradition. Mrs. W. F. Burks, who lived on a ranch near Banquete with her husband, hitched up a buggy and went along with the herd that consisted of 1,000 cows headed for Kansas. Bad weather and trouble getting cattle through timbered land around Lockhart caused the loss of twenty cows. Mrs. Burks probably tired of seeing only men and cows so when she saw an old woman sitting in the doorway of a small house in Ellis County she remarked that they had seen very few women in that area. Without missing a beat on stringing beans, the woman responded, "Yes, sir, I'm the first woman that made a track in Dallas County, and I would be back in Tennessee now, only I would have to go through Arkansas to get there. I guess I'll stay right here."[34] Actually, there were other women who made drives, but they were the exception.

In 1871 H. C. Williams, a small rancher in Refugio County, built a string of barbed wire fence for W. E. and Tom McCampbell on a place of theirs in San Patricio County. It was the first barbed wire fence in the county.[35] It was 1881 before the Coleman-Fulton Pasture Company strung a line on some of their nearby property.[36]

One of the last drives to come out of South Texas was put together by Levi J. Harkey from the Rocky Ammons Ranch on the

Atascosa River about eighteen miles from Oakville. He put 2,000 head on the trail that ended up in Dodge City, Kansas. W. M. Shannon built large pens just outside Oakville, which stockmen used to gather cattle before hitting the trail. Shannon made a trip up the trail in 1878 with Bob Martin of Refugio County.[37]

In 1873 Andrew Nations gathered 1,500 head of stocker cattle from Sulfur Creek and the Nueces River area and started up the trail. Horses were also a saleable item up north, and in 1876 Robert Dobie and E. S. Boatwright took about 600 head to Dodge City, Kansas, despite stampedes, thunderstorms, hail, and Indian problems. They delivered the herd and headed for home.[38]

Leroy Pope was one of the first to put a herd on the trail from the area after the Civil War. He started with 2,200 big steers, none under seven years old, and all wild. A thunderstorm in Bexar County caused a stampede and it took thirty days to round them all up and get back on the trail. This was his one and only trip up the trail, saying he could do better. He could. He married and had fifteen children and was proud to say: "None of my boys have ever been sent to the penitentiary or elected to the legislature, and I think that is a pretty good showing."[39]

Thomas Welder, out of Bee County, took his stock up the trail in 1873 when he delivered one hundred mules and some horses to the mouth of the Red River in Louisiana where it took five months to sell them. Evidently the margin of profit was good because for the next five years he continued the drives of mules and horses. He and Doug Williams picked up over 4,000 one-year-old steers from Welder ranches in San Patricio and Refugio counties and headed up the trail. A freeze on the Gonzales prairies killed a number of *drags*.[40] Stampedes and severe hailstorms slowed down the drive, but they finally arrived in Indian Territory. One of the first things they saw was a sign that demanded, "One Wohaw" (cow). He paid up and finally delivered the herd to Dodge City, Kansas. They returned home by way of Kansas City, Galveston, Indianola, and Victoria.[41] In 1882 he put 400 of his cattle with 5,000 belonging to J. J. Welder in San Patricio County for another drive. A stampede every night for twelve nights slowed things down, but they made Dodge City, Colorado, in June where J. J. Welder sold most of his beef to the government for use by the Indians. They worked their way up the

Arkansas River and finally delivered the last to the Kit Carson Ranch on the Union Pacific twenty miles above Denver.[42]

Alfred Iverson "Babe" Moye of Kenedy was introduced to violence when a young man by the name of Silvers was killed by the sheriff in Helena, Karnes County. Shortly afterward he saw the gory scene of the murder of the Stringfield family. Probably seeking to get away he signed on with an outfit to pick up a herd above Uvalde and take them north to Kansas. Looking for horses, the young man found a bunch of Indians that chased him back, flinging arrows at him all the way. They started the 1,500 cattle and soon arrived at the Red River after fighting off Indians trying to steal their horses at night. Upon arriving at Abilene, Kansas, the young cowpoke who left Helena because of murders, discovered the town was full of gunslingers like John Wesley Hardin, Buffalo Bill Thompson, Manny Clements, and Gip Clements. After losing all of his money gambling in the Bull Head Saloon, which was run by Thompson and Hill Coe, City Marshall Wild Bill Hickok offered the cowboy some good advice—"leave it alone." The next year he signed on with Choate & Bennett. He finally signed on with W. G. Butler, and together with his brother, Andy Moye, they got into trouble in Ogallala and had to leave in a hurry.[43] Helena looked better after each trip.

The Burnell Butler family, destined to become one of Karnes County's leading groups, came to the area in 1852 in oxcarts from Scott County, Mississippi. Oddly enough, Butler, who was deaf and dumb, did not start buying land until after the Civil War when barbed wire was invented and people started fencing their land. Up until that time it was all open range.[44] Butler settled his family close to Wafford's Crossing on the San Antonio River, and leased land on which to graze his cattle. As the Butler family and others were taming land in the area, the great drought of 1863 hit, drying the San Antonio and Nueces rivers to a trickle. Stock that roamed free, unfettered by fences, migrated across the Nueces River to an area west of the river where the drought had not been so severe. With most able-bodied men serving in the Confederate Army, work on cattle ranges came to a standstill. In 1864 the drought was broken and a group of about forty-five young and old men, headed by Uncle Billy Ricks of Oakville, spent a month in the trans-Nueces area, headquartered at San Diego, rounding up their branded cattle and their calves. About 500 head were returned to Karnes County ranges. By 1868 W. G. Butler took a herd of cattle up the trail to Abilene, Kansas, marking a return to near normal conditions in Karnes County. During the next decade he put a number of drives on the trail and increased his herds and land to over 100,000 acres, plus an additional 25,000 leased, on which he ran 10,000 head of cattle. His last drive was in 1886 and up until that time he participated in one to three drives each year. It has been estimated that he delivered over 100,000 head of cattle up the trail. P. B. Butler joined his brother in drives in the years 1874, 1875, and 1876. In 1878 P. B. Butler endured storms and trail problems to deliver 3,500 head to Dodge City, Kansas. One of his last drives was in 1879 when he took a herd of 3,500 head to Nebraska, holding them between the North and South Platte Rivers until all were sold.[45]

All drives from the area originated in Round Pens, just west of Kenedy, where the ranchers had built rail fences that encompassed acres and acres of land where cattle could be held until the herd was ready to move.

The cattle drives during and after the Civil War contributed greatly to the survival of people in the area in the postwar period. Men like Bill Butler and Monroe Choate, who organized and led most of the drives out of the area, were largely responsible for gathering, organizing, and financing these drives. Much needed employment kept idle hands busy and until the railroad came to the area in the mid-1880s the cattle drives were practically the only source of income. "These men were great," Mrs. Charlotte Nichols reminisced, "but it was the women who were the glue that kept families and communities together. That's how Karnes County survived."

No doubt the Butler family, especially William Green Butler, had a profound influence on the cattle business in South Texas. In fact, he put his stamp on Karnes County in many ways. Perhaps Mrs. Nichols, a member of the Butler family, best described the role that Bill Butler played in the troubled times in Karnes County.

> The Civil war had a big influence on his life. When he got back to Karnes County times were rough—No law, no order to anything. He, with his military training, took it upon himself to help with the law and order in Karnes County. He was very definite in his views in what was right and wrong. If you did right it was fine,

and if you did wrong it was too bad. He killed twenty some odd people, but he was always acquitted at court trials by pleading self defense. He told his grandson that there was only one person that he regretted killing. He had taken a herd of cattle to Indianola and was on the way back with his pockets full of gold. He saw this man approaching him and he didn't know what he wanted—he wouldn't stop coming—I had to shoot that man because I didn't know what he was going to do. He must have been a domineering character, positive and a firm believer in what was right and wrong. He was a leader. He became one of the roughest men in Karnes County. Later he started buying property—he owned half of Karnes County and the Nichols the other half. He would buy the property for back taxes.[46]

Bill Butler's first cattle drive was during the Civil War. His superior found out that he was a rancher and knew where herds of cattle could be found, so he sent him to Karnes County where he rounded up 500 head of cattle and headed them back toward Arkansas to feed the hungry Confederate soldiers. This was at a time when the Yankees were overrunning the area and about the time he arrived at his base the Yankees captured it[47] and the herd of cattle and took Butler as a prisoner. He and several other men were ordered to stack the captured rifles, but they just kept on walking and escaped.[48]

Cattlemen in Guadalupe County organized drives to California and New Orleans in the 1850s to find markets for their cattle who were increasing fast on the open range.[49] L. B. Anderson made his first trip up the trail in 1871. Through the years he went up the trail eighteen times, two times as a hand before being made trail boss, and sixteen more in charge. He had learned the trade well on regular "cow hunting" expeditions. Several times a year from ten to twenty men would gather and round up all of the cattle belonging to their group, returning to old man Gus Konda's place where they were divided up by Konda, John Oliver, Frank Delaney, Dud Tom, Whit Vick, W. C. Irvin, John and Dud Jefferson, Pinkney Low and sons, and Gen. William Saffold. Anderson took a drive up the trail each year until 1887. He had brushes with Indians, saw Wild Bill Hickock when he killed Phil Coe in Abilene, Kansas, on the street, and was in Newton, Kansas, when Jim Martin from Helena, Karnes County, was gunned down. Anderson spent his entire life in the cattle business.[50]

Abel Head "Shanghai" Pierce comes close to embodying the images of the rough, tough, free-wheeling cattle baron of South Texas. Perhaps his penchant for outlandish and brazen deals and lifestyle made him a legend in his time. For instance, he roamed the area from Matagorda County westward buying cattle. He was a large man who rode a fine horse and was always accompanied by a Negro boy who led a pack animal loaded with gold and silver. When he concluded a deal to buy a man's herd he would spread a wagon sheet on the ground and dump out the gold and silver[51]—he paid on the spot and ranchers strapped for cash left smiling with money in their pockets. He put together herds before the Civil War, sending some to New Orleans to Indianola for shipment to Cuba. When drives started up the trails in 1867 he gathered cattle from Live Oak, Bee, Goliad, Jackson, and Lavaca.[52] As previously mentioned, Shanghai is also credited with being among the first, along with Al McFadden and A. P. Borden, to bring Brahman cattle to South Texas in an endeavor to beat ear ticks. Shanghai and his brother John E. Pierce developed the port of Tidehaven on the Tres Palacios River and at one time had a contract with Spain to furnish cattle during their struggle to hold on to Cuba. Later a packery was located there to process cattle.[53]

Shanghai wanted to make sure he was remembered after he died so he had a life-size marble statue made of himself mounted on top of a marble base. He left instructions to be buried in its shadow. Probably some individual who had never been able to get the best of Shanghai appeared one day, and after a bit of blasphemy, fired a couple of shots at the statue. Check for yourself—Hawley Cemetery off Highway 35 near Blessing.

Victoria County had many large cattlemen but near the end of the cattle drives A. Levi & Co. of Victoria, a group of merchants and bankers, gathered a herd of 2,500 head along the Guadalupe River and hired Arthur Burns.[54] Burns made a number of other drives out of DeWitt County where he lived. His brother, J. C. Burns, later was an attorney and county judge in Goliad County. Arthur Burns, his grandfather, was a DeWitt colonist and his father, Columbus Burns, was also a trail driver, taking his first herd up the trail from DeWitt County in 1880.[55]

Goliad County furnished its share of trail drivers. Col. Dillard R. Fant entered the cattle drive business in 1886 near its end, but is

credited with taking at least 200,000 head up the trail, mainly to
Kansas, Nebraska, and Wyoming. The size of his operation can be
measured by the fact that his cattle drives required 1,200 saddle
horses and 200 men to handle the herds and supplies.[56]

Thomas Hodges, brother-in-law of Fant, recollects his father
moving one of the largest herds in the area from New Caney to
Goliad in 1838. He soon had one of the largest operations in the
area. Indians, especially during a full moon, killed a lot of cattle as
well as "quite a number" of settlers.[57]

Capt. J. D. Reed was one of the first Goliad County ranchers
to drive cattle to Powder Horn (Indianolia) for shipment to
Louisiana. Later he put large herds on the trail for Kansas before
moving to Fort Worth and then New Mexico.[58]

Two of Goliad County's largest ranchers were W. A. "Buck"
Pettus and William J. Lott. Pettus married Myra Lott, William's
daughter, to unite the two families that still live in Goliad County
today. Lott made a total of eight trips up the trail, the last in 1882
with 1,500 head. Pettus moved to one of his ranches in Bee County.
He had a reputation of having never branded a maverick calf and
was noted for his fierce drive to catch and rout out cattle thieves
and rustlers. His banner year was in 1886-87 when his herd numbered about 10,000.[59]

George Saunders came to Goliad County in 1850 with his family at age four, settling on Lost Creek which was about twelve miles
west of Goliad. They were starting from scratch and took a herd of
cattle from William Rupe for every third calf. The family was pro-
gressing when the Civil War took the father and older boys for service. By the time the war ended the local range was full of cattle that
had drifted in from East Texas and Louisiana. The post-Civil War
period brought outlaws and crooks into the area. Texas Rangers
were called into the area several times. Most of the cattle were sold
to Foster and Allen, Shanghai Pierce, or Jose Collins, who were
shipping out of Powder Horn. Mr. Saunders drove one herd from
Goliad to New Orleans in 1867. George made his first trip up the
trail at age seventeen with Monroe Choate of Karnes County.[60]

9.
THE CART ROAD AND THE CART WAR

Born to meet the demands of the thousands of families who landed in Lavaca and Indianola, the Cart Road snaked its way across several hundred miles of Raw Frontier into the promised land that would provide new homes for some and lonely graves for others. Literally thousands of early settlers died while making the trip from the coast to their inland homes. Graves were common along the trail and at camping stops. They were primarily victims of cholera and yellow fever; however, some were victims of Indian depredations.

It was sometimes called the Old Freighter Road, but it was generally referred to as the Cart Road,[1] named after the so-called Cart War of 1857 that brought the focus of the entire nation to the trail. Beginning on Lavaca Bay at Indianola or Lavaca, the trail wound its way through present-day Calhoun, Victoria, Goliad, Karnes, Wilson, and Bexar counties into San Antonio via Goliad Street. For the German settlers who were bound as far north as Fredericksburg, the journey was resumed after taking time to rest oxen and replenish supplies.[2]

From Indianola the road moved in a westward direction, dodging marshland along the coast by Chocolate Bayou to Green Lake, which afforded the travelers a good place to camp and an opportunity to organize and replenish their fresh water supply. Leaving there

105

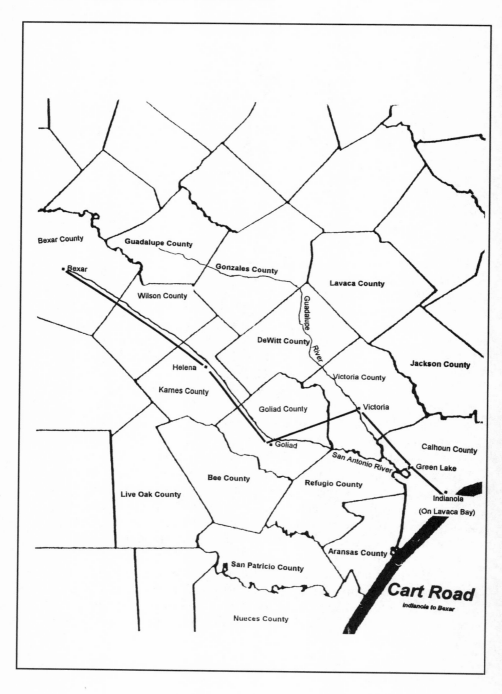

the carts followed the east bank of the Guadalupe River to Victoria where a ferry operated at a crossing[3] that could be forded when the river was not in flood stage. Goliad or La Bahia, on the San Antonio River, was the next major campground before heading north toward Runge. According to Frank Wishert, a veteran cart driver from Karnes County, the road crossed the Cibolo Creek at El Fuerte Del Cibolo[4] at the Carvajal Crossing to head north along the San Antonio River, passing through Helena and on to Floresville before entering San Antonio, or Bexar as it was called in the early days. The main route of the trail branched off at Victoria and came in a more direct route to the Cibolo crossing. The route out of Goliad also crossed at the Cibolo, thus bringing the trail back together. "I wagoned a heap. I never drove nothing but ox teams. I quit when mules come in. I never had no use for a mule," Wishert said.[5]

Depending upon the weather, the journey from Indianola to Bexar could take four to six weeks. The Mexican two-wheeled carts came in a variety of shapes and sizes, with wheels that were sometimes cut from the trunk of a single large tree. Other wheels were made with two layers of heavy hand-hewn planks held together with wooden pegs and strips of rawhide. The smaller carts could be pulled by one yoke of oxen, while the longer and heavier carts had two to four yokes of oxen. Most of the carts were driven by their Mexican owners. The Mexicans also operated lumbering wagons drawn by ten to twelve mules. Wishert put the trail in perspective:

As there is such a vast amount of goods to be hauled we can see *the road* kept hot by the tread of the feet. There are some two thousand carts owned and driven by Mexicans and drawn by three or four yokes of oxen. There are also the Mexican mule teams made up of great lumbering wagons, each with from ten to twelve mules. Besides these there are the clumsy American wagons hitched to five or six yokes of the biggest and longest horned oxen in the world. All these slow moving vehicles, constantly crawling one after the other in a steady stream, remind me of a great cloud of smoke that seems to be winding and worming its way along this road. Day after day, month after month, year after year, this great serpent keeps crawling on over the hills and prairies past our town *Helena*, along the river's edge, and onward, to finally disgorge itself in the coming city that lies to the north and west of us, San Antonio.[6]

Oxen-drawn overland freighter, 1868.
—Photo courtesy Institute of Texan Cultures.

American freight haulers usually used wagons drawn by eight or ten mules, in addition to oxen, depending on the size of the wagon and the weight of the load. Some were individually owned and others were owned by companies that had hundreds of freight wagons and hired the drivers.

The difficult time in the lives of new settlers was compounded in the mid-1850s when intense rivalry between the Mexican cart drivers and the Texian wagon drivers erupted into shooting incidents and lynching parties. Hatred left over from the Texas War for Independence, made worse by the Mexican War, heated up when Mexican cart drivers began cutting rates to haul freight from Indianola to San Antonio. American freighters were charging as much as three dollars per hundred pounds for delivery of goods from the coast to San Antonio. Merchants in San Antonio, trying to cut their costs, began hiring Mexican cart drivers at a lower rate to deliver goods. American drivers, idled by these cutrate practices, began reacting violently against the Mexican drivers. Looters, looking only for profit, also entered into the brew to make things worse.[7]

As this tempest began to explode, still another factor entered the troubled scene. In 1856 a plot was discovered among slaves in Colorado County to murder their masters and head for the Mexican border. This was a well-organized effort that had gathered up a collection of arms. In Matagorda County young Mexican men were stealing Negro girls for their wives and running away with them. This advanced to the point that a law was passed in the county making it illegal for Mexicans to reside in the area. Prejudice against Mexicans was rampant and open warfare along the Cart Road became a way of life. Mexicans were accused of helping the Negro slaves escape to Mexico where they would be free. Mexicans were also accused of butchering cattle along the trail for their own use, much to the anger of ranchers. Whole families frequently followed the Mexican cart trains, living off the road. This gave the ranchers and white freighters common cause to try and drive the Mexican cart drivers from the road.[8]

As early as April of 1855 a committee of vigilance was formed in Guadalupe County to keep the Mexicans out of the county. Mexican carts were destroyed in the Seguin area. Emotions ran high on both sides, giving rise to the possibility of a race war. In July of 1857 six Mexicans were wounded and one American killed when armed bands of unknown race attacked in three different places. It was speculated that the Know Nothing Party was behind the movement.[9]

Legends tell that the Hanging Tree on the square in Goliad was the site of the hanging of two *braceros* (instigators of the Cart War) early in 1857. Unconfirmed stories list as many as nine Mexican cart operators who were swung from this tree. Other stories, backed only by legends, tell that the lynching fever also spilled over to as

Mule-drawn wool train.
—Photo courtesy Institute of Texan Cultures.

Indians attacking a wagon train.
—Photo courtesy Institute of Texan Cultures.

many as twenty horse and cattle thieves who were caught plying their trade.[10]

A meeting was held in Goliad that proclaimed: "We declare the sentiment of this meeting, and we believe of the whole people to be that the continuance of the greasers or peon Mexicans as citizens among us is an intolerable nuisance and a grievance which calls loudly for redress."[11]

A writer in Helena described the situation in this manner: "Another favorite sport of the natives was looting the great freight wagons carrying goods from Indianola to San Antonio." Evidently the none-too-scrupulous people of Helena felt justified in stealing from all freighters as long as bad feelings existed between the Texian and the Mexican drivers.

American freighters in the Helena area also slipped into Mexican camps at night and cut the spokes of the wagon wheels so that the wagon would crash the next morning when they started. This led to shootings and Mexican deaths. A battle took place on

CHAPTER 9: THE CART ROAD AND THE CART WAR   111

Cibolo Creek in Karnes County. The Mexican carts and American wagons formed two giant hollow circles and fired away at each other. No lives were lost, but evidently the Mexicans accepted the fact that they were beaten and retired, leaving the trade to the Americans.

In September of 1857 a train of seventeen carts, under the leadership of W. G. Tobing, headed out of San Antonio and was attacked near Helena by a group of men with blackened faces. Two Mexicans were killed and a number wounded, and one American attacker was wounded. There were other murders and goods stolen from Mexican carts. San Antonio merchants raised such a howl that Maj. Gen. D. E. Twiggs began offering escorts to wagon trains, mainly those carrying government supplies. This did not stop the trouble and a mob headed by Colonel Wilcox appeared and threatened to sack the town of Helena. A lynching party was narrowly avoided. Feelings of the people of Karnes County exploded in a public meeting held on December 4, 1857, at the Helena courthouse to consider the Cart War and the meddling of Governor E. M. Pease, mentioned above. John J. Linn, a Victoria merchant and a hero at the Battle of San Jacinto, had these terse words concerning the warfare on the Cart Road: "The authorities of Goliad County seemed to regard the whole thing with supine indifference, as they made no efforts whatever either to suppress the crimes or to bring the criminals to justice." Lynch law took over. During the height of the trouble the Mexican drivers made a new road out of Goliad that ran twelve to fifteen miles to the left of the main road for a short distance.[12]

A train of carts loaded with United States government supplies was attacked in Karnes County on September 12, 1857. One Mexican cartman was killed and several wounded.[13]

Governor Pease finally called out a company of seventy-five men to put an end to the Cart War after the matter was aired in the legislature. No doubt the complaint lodged by the Mexican minister in October of 1857 to federal authorities influenced Pease's action.[14]

The problem did not go away over night. The *Houston Telegraph and Register* weighed into the Cart War with several pronouncements. One article on December 19, 1857, expressed their opinions: "There is evidently a large amount of prejudice existing among our people against the greaser population, which often breaks out in acts of violence and lawlessness, altogether indefensible." Again on January 10,

1858 the paper reported on the meeting held earlier in Karnes County: "They don't like the 'means' the governor has provided for the purpose, troops traveling with wagon trains, and authorized their representatives to oppose the payment of the troops he [the governor] has employed." On October 18, 1858, the *Nueces Valley* of Corpus Christi reported that General Twiggs furnished a military escort to accompany the Mexican teamsters and protect the government stores from San Antonio to Indianola.

Perhaps the Mexicans received relief from Governor Pease and through the intervention of the Mexican minister[15] at Washington, but to a large extent Mexican cart drivers retired from the scene. The American wagon trains dominated the road until such time as the railroad retired them to museums.

APPENDICES

Old Eighteen

The only defenders left in Gonzales on September 29, 1835 were:

William W. Arrington	George W. Davis	Capt. Albert Martin
Simon Bateman	Almoron Dickerson	Charles Mason
Valentine Bennett	Graves Fulchear	Thomas R. Miller
Joseph D. Clements	Benjamin Fuqua	John Sowell
Almond Cottle	James B. Hinds	Winslow Turner
Jacob C. Darst	Thomas Jackson	Ezekial Williams

Forty-Two Gonzales Men Who Died at the Alamo

Source for Gonzales Men: Gonzales County Historical Commission, *History of Gonzales County*, Texas, (Dallas: Curtis Media Corporation, 1986), 32, 33; Ethel Zivley Rather, "DeWitt's Colony," *Southwest Historical Quarterly*, 8:154.

Col. William Travis issued his appeal for help, and when it reached Gonzales twenty-two men started immediately in relief. On the way ten more joined, bringing the number to thirty-two. They were:

Isaac Baker	Dolphin Ward Floyd	William P. King
John Cane (Cain)	Galva Fuqua	Jonathan L. Lindley
George Cottle	John E. Garvin	Capt. Albert Martin
David Cummings	John E. Gaston	Jesse McCoy
Squire Damon (Daymon)	James George	Thomas Miller
Jacob Darst	Thomas Jackson	Isaac Milsap
John Davis	Johnny Kellogg	George Neggan
William Dearduff	Andrew Kent	William E. Summers
Charles Despallier	George C. Kimball	George W. Tumlinson
William Fitzbauch	(Kimble)	Robert White
(Fishbaugh)	John G. King	Claiborne Wright
John Flanders		

Gonzales researchers have established since 1936 that John G. King was ill at home during this period and it was his son, William P. King, who died in the Alamo.

Others from Gonzales who were already at the Alamo were:

Daniel Bourne	Andrew Duval	William J. Lightfoot
George Brown	John Harris	Amos Pollard
Jerry C. Day	James McGee	Marcus L. Sewell
Almoron Dickerson		

Thirty-one men from Gonzales County followed Gen. Sam Houston and fought in the Battle of San Jacinto. They were:

Moses Baker	James Hinds	William Pettus
George W. Davis	James Hughes	Jesse Robinson
James P. Davis	Joseph Kent	James Shaw
Jesse Kencheloe Davis	John McCoy	Samuel Shupe
John Davis	John McCrabb (McCrab)	Robert Smith
Edward Dickinson	Charles Mason	George Sutherland
Horace Eggleston	Spencer Morris	Josiah Taylor
John Ferrell	James D. Owen	William Taylor
William S. Fisher	Nicholas Peck	John James Tumlinson
John Hallett	Edward C. Pettus	Andrew Zumwalt
William Hill		

Men in Dimmitt's Command

List compiled by Hobart Huson and used in
Captain Philip Dimmitt's Commandancy of Goliad.

> *Symbols:*
>
> C: Collinsworth Capture
> Dec: Signer Goliad Declaration
> DG: Dimmitt's Garrison
> Fannin: Fannin's Command
> JG: Johnson and Grant
> Lip. Exp: Lipantitlan Expedition
> R: Battle at Refugio
>
> RAL: Reinforcement of Alamo
> Sg A: Siege of the Alamo
> Sg Bx: Siege of Bexar
> St Bx: Storming of Bexar
> Tx N: Texas Naval Service
> ?: Probable service

Adams, Thomas Jefferson, C, DG, FC, SJ
Aldrete, Jose Miguel (Refugio Colonist), C?, DG, GD
Aldrete, Trinidad (Refugio Colonist), C?, DG, GD
Allison, Alfred, C, DG
Amador, Juan, patriot, courier, C?, DG?
Anderson, Thomas, C, DG, SJ
Armstrong, H. F., C
Atkinson, Milton B., C? DG, Sg Bx, St Bx, SJ.

Baker, O., (John Andrew Baumacher) C, DG
Barton, Jefferson A., C, SJ
Baylor, John Walker, C, DG, Sg Bx, St Bx, Dec, S (also member of Horse Marines)
Bell, J. T., DG, St Bx, Dec
Bell, Thos. B, Sg Bx, St Bx, Dec, SJ
Benavides, Eugenio, Patriot
Benavides, Capt. Placedo, Alcalde of Victoria, C, Sg Bx, St Bx, JG
Bennett, Caleb, C, DG, Fannin

Bennett, James, DG, SJ

Bennett, Valentine, (?), Sg Bx

Blair, Samuel, (Refugio Colonist), DG, St Bx, Sg A

Blake, Thomas M., C, DG, Fannin

Borden, John Petti, C, DG, (2nd Lt.), St Bx, SJ

Bowen, John (Refugio Colonist), DG, St Bx, Dec

Bower, John White (San Pat Colonist), Capt. of Spy Co., cooperated with Dimmitt's Garrison, Fannin, signer Tex. Dec. Ind.

Bowman, John J., C, DG, Sg Bx, Dec

Bowman, Joseph, DG, Dec (2nd Sgt.)

Brown, James, (Refugio Colonist), DG, Sg Bx, died at Alamo

Brown, William S., (Sea Captain), designer of Bloody Arm Sword Flag, DG, Sg Bx, Dec, Tx N, St Bx

Brush, Elkanah, (Refugio Colonist), C, DG, Lip Exp, Dec, His sons, Gilbert and Bradford also may have served with Dimmitt

Burke, James, (Refugio Colonist), DG, Dec

Byrne, Matthew, (Refugio Colonist), DG, Fannin.

Cadle, Joseph, C, DG, Capt. Artillery

Cannon, Thomas, C

Carbajal, Jose M. Jesus, (Afterwards General), after escape from Monclova to Texas to Victoria, cooperated with Dimmitt

Carbajal, Manuel, C. DG, St Bx?, Dec

Carbajal, Mariano, C, DG, St Bx, Dec, Fannin

Carleton, Dr. William, C, DG, Lip Exp, Sg Bx

Carlisle, Robert, (Refugio Colonist), Committee to organize militia

Cash, George W., merchant trader of Goliad and participated in the capture and purveyed to Garrison. He was killed at Coleto. His heirs received certificate for his service from Oct. 9 to March 27

Cash, John L., young son of above was also in fight at Coleto but was released to die years later in the Black Bean Lottery

Castlow, William, Dimmitt signed a certificate of his service from Oct. 9, 1835 to January 9, 1836

Caton _____. This name, without the given one, appears on several of Dimmitt's rosters

Chalwell, Gustavus (Cholwell) appears to have been an early member and also a signer

Collinsworth, Captain George Morse, commander of expedition which captured Goliad on Oct. 9-10, 1835. He was the first pro tem commandant of the garrison which shortly became Dimmitt's

Collinsworth, Lt. David C., of the Expedition and 1st of Dimmitt's Garrison, and the first of the garrison to die violently. He is buried at Goliad.

Canstanta, A., Victoria, member of Collinsworth Expedition

Cummings, Wiley (William), DG

Dale, Joseph Benjamin, (Refugio Colonist), DG, St Bx, JG

Davis, H. F. (Oscar), C, DG, Dec

Day, Jeremiah, Sr., (Refugio Colonist), C, was on DG

Day, Jeremiah, Jr., (Refugio Colonist)

DeLeon, Sylvestre, C, St Bx, Sg Bx

Dennis, Thomas Mason, (Matagorda Colonist), DG, Dec, SJ

Despallier, Charles M., DG, St Bx, Dec, Sg A

Devereaux, Andrew, (Refugio Colonist), C, DG, Dec

Dietrich, Francis, (Refugio Colonist). His name does not appear in any roster I have seen. He was a merchant trader who received a "family" HR along with Baumaker and Langenheim who served with Dimmitt

Dimmitt, Philip, (Commandant), C, DG, St Bx, Dec, RAL

Dooley, Spirse, C, DG, Dec

Duncan, James, C, DG, Dec, Fannin

Duncan, John, (Sea Captain), C, SJ

Dunn, John (Refugio Colonist), *Alcalde*, Com. Safety, DG 10-10-1835 to 1-10-1836.

Elder, James, DG, Dec

Erwin, Dr. Thomas R., C, DG (Surgeon), Sg Bx, St Bx

Escalera, Manuel, D, Dg, (Scout), St Bx

Espalier, Carlos, C, Dg, (Scout)

Fagan, James W., DG (Commissary), Fannin

Fagan, Nicholas, D, DG, Dec

Fagen, John, C, DG (commissary), Fannin

Falcon, Raymond, C

Fitzgerald, Edward W. B., DG, Dec

Flick, John, C, SJ

Fox, Michael, DG

Fraser, Hugh McDonald, C, DG, Fannin, SJ.

Galvan, Roberto, C, Provisioner

Galvan, Tomas (St. Sp. Army Rtd.), Provisioner

Garcia, Francisco, C. DG (Scout)

Garza, Marcelo de la, DG (Scout and hauling), Sg Bx, Fannin

Garza, Paulino de la, DG (Scout and hauling), Sg Bx, Fannin

Gates, Lucius W. (Refugio Colonist), C, DG, Fannin

George, David, C., DG, Dec

George, Holman, C?, DG, Dec

George Jefferson, C, DG, Horton's, Fannin

George, Thomas, C, DG, Dec

Gould (EE) William, (Refugio Colonist), DG, Dec

Graves, Ransom O., C, DG, Dec, Fannin

Haddon, Henry, C, DG

Haddon, William, C, DG, Dec, Fannin (escaped from massacre)

Hall, John W., C, SJ

Ham, John, C

Hamilton, Thomas, C, DG (died in service Nov. 23, 1835)

Hancock, John P. (F), DG, (2nd Sgt.), Dec

Hannum, James, DG (died Dec. 14, 1835 as per roster)

Hanson, Thomas, DG, Dec, SJ

Hart, Timothy, (Refugio Colonist), DG

Hearn, Robert Patrick, (Refugio colonist), C, DG, Battle of Refugio, Horse Marines

Hews (Hughes), James, (Refugio Colonist), D, Westover, Fannin

Hicks, Milton, D, DG, Sg Bx

Hill, William G., C, Sg Bx, St Bx, DG, Dec

Holbrook, Nathaniel, (Refugio Colonist), C, DG, Dec

Howe, Dr. Joseph (Surgeon to Dimmitt, Nov. 1835), DG, Dec, (Surgeon to Fannin)

Howth, William E., Sg Bx, St Bx, (Capt.) DG, Dec

Huff, John, DG, Fannin

Hutchings, J. C., DG, Dec

Hynes, John, DG, Fannin

Hynes, Peter, DG, Dec

Ingram, Allen, Sg Bx, St Bx, DG? Fannin, SJ

Ingram, Ira, C, DG, Dec, Matagorda Vols., Sutherland Co.

James, John, (Refugio Colonist), Sindinco, C, DG, Dec, Westover, Fannin

Johnson, John, (Sea Capt.) DG, Dec, SJ

Jones, Augustus H., C, (1st. Lt.) DG, Sg Bx, Dec?, St Bx

Jones, D.M., DG, Dec

Jones, Francis, C., DG, Dec, Horton.

Keating, John (Refugio Colonist), C, DG, (St Fraser)

Keller, F. R., (F.G.), C, DG

Kelly, Charles, (Refugio Colonist)?

Kelly, James (Refugio Colonist), ?

Kelly, John (Refugio Colonist), ?

Kelly, Michael, DG, Dec

Kerr, James, DG, (Advisor), Lip. Exp.

Kilpatrick (Kirkpatrick), J. Dodd, DG, Surgeon, Dec, Flag Independence.

Labaltrier, Charles?, SJ

Lambert, Nicholas?

Lambert, Walter, (Refugio Colonist), nephew of Col. Power and 17 year old veteran, SJ, C, DG, St Bx, Dec., Fannin

Langenheim, William, (Refugio Colonist), C, Sg Bx, JG

Lawler, Martin, (Refugio Colonist), C, DG

Lentano (See Zenteno, post)

Lightfoot, William D., (Wm J.), C, DG, Sg Bx, St Bx, SJ

Linn, John Joseph, (Padrino), DG, Lip Exp

Living, William H., (Sea Capt.), DG, St Bx, Dec, Tx N

Loupy, Victor Armand, (Refugio Colonist), C, DG, St Bx, SJ

Lynch, Dr. Alexander, Surgeon, DG, Dec.

Maine, George Washington, Citizen of Refugio, not shown on DG, hero of Alamo

Malone, Charles, (Refugio Colonist), DG, Dec

Malone, John, (Refugio Colonist), Com. Safety, DG, Dec

Martindale, Daniel, C, DG, Fannin, Horton's

McAuley, Malcolm, (Refugio Colonist), reputedly DG

McCafferty, Edward, (San Pat Colonist), Dec, Died in Alamo

McClure, Robert, DG, Dec

McCullough, L. (or S), Negro Freedman, C, Sg Bx, St Bx, Legislative Citation

McDonough, Edward, (Refugio Colonist), C?, DG, Dec, Fannin

McDonough, Hames, (son of Edward), reputedly DG

McDonough, Joyn, (son of Edward), reputedly DG

McFarlane, Dugald, C, DG, Lt, Dec

McGloin, John, (San Pat Colonist), DG, Sg Bx

McKnight, George, (Refugio Colonist), DG, Fannin

McMinn, Hugh, DG, Dec

Mercer, R.C.

Messer, Charles, C, DG, Dec

Milam Benjamin Rush, C, Sg Bx, St Bx

Mitchell, Thomas, (Physician-Apothecary), C, DG, Dec, St Bx, JG

Moore, James W., C (1st Lt.), Horton, Fannin

Morris, George, (Refugio Colonist), DG, SJ

Morris, Henry J., DG, Dec.

Neven, Patrick, (San Pat Colonist), joined Westover, Fannin

New, William Jackson, C

Newland, William, C, DG, Dec

Noble, Benjamin J., DG, (1st Lt.), Dec, RAL, Horton

Nowland (Nowlin), James, DG, St Bx, RAL, Alamo Victim

O'Boyle, Andrew, (San Pat Colonist), may have served later with DG, Westover, Fannin

O'Brien, Morgan, Andrew, John and Thomas, Hugh?, nephews of James Power reputedly served with Dimmitt (Not shown on muster rolls or Declaration)

O'Connor, Charles James (Sea Capt.), C, DG, St Bx, Dec. SJ?

O'Connor, James, (Refugio Colonist), C, DG, Dec, SJ? (See Charles James O'Connor). This James served at SJ in Calder's company with Thomas O'Connor, who had brother Thomas

O'Connor, Thomas, (Refugio Colonist), was the seventeen-year-old nephew of Col. James Power, C, DG, Dec, Fannin, SJ?, (Calder's Company)

Odem (O'dem) David, Appears to have served with Dimmitt's Garrison, but not so shown on extant rolls. He was in Battle SJ

O'Leary, Patrick, DG, Dec

O'Reilly, Michael, D, Dec

O'Toole (See Toole, post)

Padilla, Jose Antonio, C, Sg Bx, St Bx, Texas Patriot

Paine, George W. (Payne), C, DG, Dec, Horton, Fannin

Parker, Christopher, DG, Sg Bx, Alamo

Peeks, H. H., DG, Dec

Perkins, B. H., DG, Dec (Major Perkins?)

Perry, Edward, (Refugio Colonist), scout, Fraser Spy Co., escaped massacre

Pollan (Polan), James, (Refugio Colonist), DG, Dec, Fraser, SJ (killed)

Pollan (Polan), Jasper, (Refugio Colonist)
Pollan (Polan) John, (Refugio
    Colonist), C, DG, Dec, Fraser, SJ
Portilla, Capt Felipe Roque de la,
    father-in-law to Colonel Power,
    adviser and purveyor to DG
Portilla, Francisco de la (son of above),
    guide to Lipantitlan Exp., killed by
    Indians during war
Powell, Lewis, DG, Dec, Horton, Fannin
Power, Colonel James, Empresario
    Refugio Colony, on Dimmitt's
    Council, Lip. Exp.
Power, Martin, (nephew of Col. Power,
    cripple), Alcalde, served with Dimmit
Pratt, William, DG, Dec.
Quinn, James, (Refugio Colonist),
    DG, Dec, 1st Lt. Tex. Army
Quinn, Edmond (Edward), (Refugio
    Colonist), DG, Dec, Fraser, SJ
Quinn, Patrick, (Refugio Colonist), C,
    DG, Fannin
Quirk, Edmond, (Refugio Colonist),
    DG, Dec, Fraser, SJ
Rawls (Rawles), Benjamin, C, DG, Dec
Rawls (Rawles), James, Dimmitt's
    Cert. enlistment, C, DG, on
    Dimmitt's Roll 2-31-1836
Redding, Robert L., C, DG (Lt.),
    St Bx, Dec
Redding, William G., C, DG, St Bx, Dec
Redfield, William, DG, Dec
Reed, Thomas, J., C
Reiley, Michael, (Refugio Colonist), DG
Robertson, William, (Refugio
    Colonist), DG, Dec, SJ?
St. John, Edward (Edmund), C, DG, Dec
St. John, James, DG, Dec
St. John, William, DG, Dec, (he was a
    teenager)
Sayle, (Silerst), Siley, C, DG (gunsmith),
    Dec, Fannin, Battle at Refugio,
    spared, but later shot at Goliad
Scott, A., (Old Caney, Collinsworth)
Scott, James W., C, DG, Dec
Scott, Thomas, (Refugio Colonist), DG
Seguin, Erasmo, provisioner to
    Dimmitt's Garrison
Shearn, Charles, (Refugio Colonist),
    G, DG, Dec

Shearn, John (teenage son of above),
    C, DG, Dec
Shelly, John (Refugio Colonist), DG, Dec
Shelly, Patrick, (son of above, possibly
    teenager)
Shingle, Charles, DG, St Bx?, Dec (ser-
    vice continued to June 25, 1836)
Sideck (Sydeck), Antonine, (Refugio
    Colonist), generally reputed
    member DG
Sideck (Sydeck), Jean (John) Baptiste,
    (Refugio Colonist), DG, Dec,
    Fraser, Battle at Refugio, Fannin?
Silsbe (Sillsbee), Albert, C, DG, Dec
Smiley, John A., (Refugio Colonist),
    C, DG
Smith, Charles, (Refugio Colonist),
    DG, Fannin (escaped massacre)
Smith, Francis R., (P), DG, Dec
Stamans, Horace, D, DG, Dec
Stapp, Darwin M.? (signed certificate
    of service of Dr. Wm. Carleton with
    Collinsworth and Dimmitt, implying
    himself as a Collinsworth member)
Stevenson, Robert, member Collins-
    worth Expedition.
Teal, Peter, (Refugio Colonist), C, DG
Thomas, Thomas S., C, Horton, Fannin
Todd, Thomas, DG, Dec
Toole, John, (Refugio Colonist), sent to
    San Patricio with John Williams and
    made prisoner at Lipantitlan, sent to
    Mexico and supposedly died in jail.
Valentine, Henry, DG
Vasquez, Encarnacion, Alcalde Goliad,
    merchant, purveyor to Dimmitt's
    Garrison, elected delegate to
    Convention of March 1, 1836
Vasquez, J. Antonio, committee to
    organize Goliad Militia, cooperated
    with Collinsworth Expedition, DG.
Walmsley (Warmsley, Wormsby),
    James, (Refugio Colonist), DG
Ware, Jefferson, DG, Dec
Welsh (Welch), George W., DG, Sg Bx,
    St Bx, Dec
Western, Thomas G., merchant-trader,
    adviser to Dimmitt, member of com-
    mittee to treat with Indians, delegate
    from Goliad to General Council

White, Allen (Alvin E.), citizen of
Refugio, DG, Dec
White, Benj. J., (Sr.),C. DG, St Bx, Dec
White, Benj. J. (Jr.), C, DG, St Bx,
Dec, Tex. Army
Wildy (Wiley), Samuel, C, SJ
Williams, Henry, Refugio citizen, C
Williams, John, (Refugio Colonist),
sent with Toole to San Pat, cap-
tured, escaped, joined Fannin and
escaped massacre
Williams, Napoleon Bonaparte, C,
DG, Dec, Horton, massacred with
Fannin's men

Wilson, David, DG, St Bx, Dec, died at
Alamo
Winningham, A., DG, Dec
Winningham, William S., DG, Dec,
Westover, Goliad Massacre
Woodward, Alvin D., DG, St Bx, Dec
Woodward, William, DG, Dec
Wooten, Edward B., C, Sg Bx
Zenteno (Zantano), (Lantero),
(Lanteno), Juan, customs collector
of Goliad who collaborated with
Dimmitt and Kerr in the capture of
Goliad.

Col. Francis W. Johnson's Command
at Battle of San Patricio, Feb. 27, 1836

Thirty-four men:

Killed in city of Old San Patricio:

Dr. Gustav Bunsen
Henry Coney
Benjamin Dale
Dr. William

M. W. Hort
Thomas K. Perason
William Williams

Two San Antonio Mexicans were with Johnson but their names were never
found.

Captured and sent to Matamoros:

William B. Benson
John Bryan
George Copeland
Sebastian Francois
William L. Hall

Lucius H. Kerr
William Langeheim
Phineas Jenks Mahan
Samuel W. McKneely

Thomas S. Mitchell
Hutchins M. Pittman
Thomas Robinson
John Spiess

Five San Antonio Mexicans, including Arreola and Zambranco.

Escaped:

John F. Beck
Edward H. Hufty
Francis W. Johnson

John H. Love
James M. Miller
Daniel J. Toler

Beck, Hufty, and Miller were killed at Goliad with Fannin's men. Two
other Americans are also thought to have been killed in the battle.

Dr. James Grant's Party wiped out near Agua Dulce, March 2, 1836
Party consisted of twenty-six, including three Mexicans.

Killed in ambush:

James M. Cass	Dr. Charles P. Heartt	Horace Ovid Marshall
Joseph Carpenter	J.T. Howard	John C. McLanglin
Stephen Denison	Joseph Smith Johnson	Robert C. Morris
Dr. James Grant	Thomas Lewellen	J.W. Wentworth

Captured and sent to Matamoros prison:

Ruben R. Brown	Stillman S. Curtis
John Collett	Nelson Jones

Two Mexicans are also thought to have been in this list.

Escaped:

Placido Benavides	David Moses
Randolph DeSpain	James Reed
William James Gatlin	William Scurlock

All of the escapees except Benavides joined Fannin and were killed on March 27. Scurlock was spared as a nurse. Two Americans, as yet unidentified, were also killed at Auga Dulce.

Colonel Ward's and Captain King's Men

Killed in fighting at Refugio March 14-16, 1836:

Samuel Anderson	Jesse C. Humphries	William Shelton
William S. Armstrong	William R. Johnson	William K. Simpson
Leslie G. H. Brady	Amon Butler King	Gavin H. Smith
James Henry Callison	Harvey H. Kirk	Oliver Smith
John H. Colgrove	Sneed Ledbetter	John C. Stewart
Thomas Cook	James B. Murphy	Robert A. Toler
Fields Davis	James Murphy	William Wallace
Jackson Davis	George W. Penny	John Ward
Henry H. Eadock	Anderson Ray	Thomas G. Weeks
Lewis C. Glibbs	John B. Rodgers	Christopher Winters
James Henley	Antoine Sayle	Samuel Wood
Joel F. Heth		

Captured with Captain King, but not killed:

Lewis Ayers	Charles Jenson
Francis Dieterich	Benjamin D. Odlum
Nicholas Fagan	

Abraham H. Osborn was spared by General Urrea and Colonel Holsinger. John James was captured at this time and spared, only to be killed at Goliad with Fannin.

Men lost or escaped near Victoria during Colonel Ward's retreat:

Water party sent forward March 16, 1836:

William H. Butler	Henry G. Hudson
John Bright	Hugh Rogers
O. H. Perry Davis	Richard Rutledge.
David I. Holt	

Killed in action near Victoria March 21, 1836:

Daniel B. Brooks	Seven other unknown men
Stith Cooner	were probably included in
Thomas Quirk	Refugio or Goliad lists.

Colonel Ward's command escaped on Guadalupe River, on night of March 21:

Joseph Andrews	McK. Moses
Benjamin F. Bradford	L. T. Pease
Samuel G. Hardaway	Joel D. Rains
Charles Frederick Heck	George Rounds
Allen Ingram	James P. Trezevant.

Detailed to build boats in Victoria, March 23, 1836 and escaped:

James H. Barnwell	John James Lamkin
Joseph Callaghan	James H. Neely
James H. Callaghan	John O'Daniel, Jr.
Joseph Gamble	Edward Paterson
Roderick Pierce Hammock	Thomas J. Smith
Andrew Jackson Hitchcock	John T. Spiller
Thomas Horry	Thomas G. Steward
John C. P. Kennymore	William L. Wilkinson.

Detained at Victoria by General Urrea and later escaped:

Emanuel Durain	Benjamin Mordecai
Sion Duff Greene	William Welsh.
Martin Moran	

Men of Colonel Fannin's Command
who escaped to Victoria
as of March 18-19, 1836

Silas M. Duret   Elam Ludington

Captain A. C. Horton's Cavalry
Not Captured on March 19-20

Horton's cavalry joined Fannin's command at Goliad but elected not to join Fannin's force in the battle near Coleto Creek and thus escaped the Goliad Massacre. They were:

Thomas Jefferson Adams	Nicholas W. Eastland	John L. Osborn
Norman Austin	Joseph Fenner	Thomas Osborn
Jacob Betts	William C. Francis	Leve Pendleton
Garrett E. Boom	Jefferson George	Michael Riley
George J. Bridgeman	Albert C. Horton	George N. Robinson
George Whitfield Brooks	Francis Jones	Christopher Terrell
J. W. Buckner	John Jones	Thomas S. Thompson
Thomas Cantwell	Augustus S. Kincheloe	Dr. John Walker
Joseph Clements	James W. Moore	George W. Wheelwright
Lewis DeMoss	Charles Morgan	Ralph Wright
William DeMoss		

Killed in action, or mortally wounded March 19, 1836:

Alfred Dorsey	George McKnight
Conrad Eigenauer	H. Francis Petrussewicz
John Jackson	William Guinn
John Kelly	William F. Savage
William H. Mann	Archibald Swords

Fannin's Men captured at Coleto
and ordered killed by General Santa Anna
in Goliad March 27, 1836

Wiley A. Abercrombie	Layton Allen	Allison Ames
James Moss Adams	Peter Allen	Patrick H. Anderson
Isaac Aldridge	Alfred Allison	James S. Bagby
John Aldridge	William L. Allston	Augustus Baker

Stephen Baker
John H. Barkely
John N. Barnhill
Thomas B. Barton
Anthony Bates
James S. Batts
Josias B. Beall
John F. Beck
Marvin Bell
Fred J. Bellows
Henry Hogue Bentley
Joseph H. Blackwell
Thomas M. Blake
Gabriel Bouch
Leslie G. H. Bracey
James A. Bradsford
Richard G. Brashear
John M. Brayson
Nathaniel R. Brister
John Sowers Brooks
J. S. Brown
Oliver Brown
William S. Brown
Daniel Buckley
Thomas Burbidge
Benjamin F. Burt
Moses Butler
Alfred Bynum
Matthew Byrne
J. W. Cain
Mariano Carabajal
George Washington
   Carlisle
Charles J. Carrier
Michael E. Carroll
Ewing Caruthers
George W. Cash
Joseph M. Chadwick
John Chew
Enoch P. Gains Chisum
Thomas T. Churchill
Joseph H. Clark
Steth Clark
John G. Coe
George W. Coglan
William H. Cole
Jacob Coleman
William John Colston
William Comstock
Cullen Conrad

Matthew Conway
Thomas H. Cosby
William J. Cowan
Harvey Cox
Henderson Cozart
John Cross
George W. Cumming
John D. Cunningham
George F. Curtman
George Washington
   Daniell
Thomas Jefferson Dasher
Robert T. Davidson
George A. Davis
Walter W. Daws
H. B. Day
Napoleon Debicki
George Dedrick
Joseph Dennis
Randolph DeSpain
Michael Devereaus
William P. Dickerman
Noah Dickinson, Jr.
Abijah Hogan Dickson
Henry H. Dickson
Richard Disney
John Donoho
Henry L. Douglass
William G. Douglas
Henry M. Downman
Brown Dubose
J. E. Duffield
James W. Duncan
Francis J. Dusanque
Burr H. Duval
George Dyer
Andrew H. Eddy
Samuel M. Edwards
Otis G. Eels
James E. Ellis
Michael Ellis
John Ely
Robert English
Scott George Eubanks
John Fadden
James Walker Fannin
Samuel Farney
Robert Fenner
Joseph G. Ferguson
Charles Fine

John H. Fisher
Edward Fitzsimmons
Arthur G. Foley
J. A. Foster
Bradford Fowler
Elijah B. Fanklin
Hugh McDonald Fraser
Charles Frazer
William Warren Frazer
Micajah G. Frazier
Thomas S. Freeman
Terrell R. Frizzell
Hezekiah Frost
Edward Fuller
Dominie Gallagher
David Gamble
Edward Garner
M. C. Garner
Lucius W. Gates
William James Gatlin
John Gibbs
Lewis C. Gibbs
Imanuel Frederic
   Giebenrath
William Gilbert
Francis Gilkinson
George M. Giland
John Gimble
John Gitchard
John Gleeson
John C. Grace
Ransome O. Graves
Francis H. Gray
George Green
William T. Green
James H. Grimes
E.J.D. Grinolds
____, Gould
William Gunter.
James A. Hamilton
John J. Hand
Charles S. Hardwick
William Harper
Jesse Harris
William Harris
Erasmus D. Harrison
Charles Ready Haskell
Henry Hastie
William R. Hatfield
Norborne B. Hawkins

Ebenezer Smith Heath
Wilson Helma
William Hemphill
John Heyser
Stuart Hill
Nathan Hodge
Edward H. Hufty
Wesley Hughes
Wiley Hughes
Jesse C. Humphries
Francis M. Hunt
William Hunter
Stephen Decatur Hurst
James C. Jack
John N. Jackson
John James
Charles B. Jennings
Henry W. Jones
David Johnson
Edward J. Johnson
William P. Johnson
James Kelly
John Kelly
James P. Kemp
Montgomery B. King
Allen O. Kinney
P. T. Kissam
John Kornicky
Adams G. Lamond
Charles Lantz
Green Lee
Oscar F. Leverett
Charles Linley
John C. Logan
Alexander J. Loverly
Joseph S. Loving
A. M. Lynch
A.H. Lynde
Dennis Mahoney
Henry Martin
Peter Mattern
Samuel A. J. Mays
James McCoy
James A. McDonald
John McGloin
Dennis McGowan
John McGowan
Kenneth McKenzie
Charles McKinley
Alexander McLennan

J.B. McMonomy
William McMurray
James McSherry
William Jefferson
    Merrifield
Isaac H. Miller
James M. Miller
Seaborn A. Mills
Charles C. Milne
Drury Hugh Minor
Warren Jordan Mitchell
Washington Mitchell
Claiborne D. Mixon
John Moat
Edward Moody
David Moore
John H. Moore
John O. Moore
John F. Morgan
David Moses
Charles Rufus Munson
David A. Murdock
Patrick Neven
Watkins Nobles
James Noland
John M. Oliver
Zeno R. O'Neal
Patrick Osborn
Robert Smith Owings
Robert A. Pace
George W. Paine
John K. Parker
William S. Parker
William Parvin
Charles Patton
George W. Penny
Austin Perkins
D.A.J. Perkins
William Perry
A. Adolph Petrussewiez
Overton Samuel Pettus
Rufus R. Petty
Charles Phillips
Stephen Pierce
James F. Pittman
Samuel C. Pittman
Lewis Powell
John M. Powers
William G. Preusch
Robert R. Rainey

James Reed
Thomas B. Rees
Perry Reese
Thomas Reeves
John Richards
Samuel Riddell
Joseph P. Riddle
Henry D. Ripley
Thomas H. Roberts
Cornelius Rooney
Samuel Rowe
Thomas Rumley
Edward Ryan
Samuel Smith Sanders
Wade H. Sanders
Charles Sargent
James H. Saunders
Henry Lewis Schultz
R. J. Scott
John Sealy
J.M. Seaton
Frederick Sevenman
John Seward
Fortunatus S.
    Schackelford
William J. Shackelford
Zachariah H. Schort
S. Simmons
Lawson S. Simpson
Randolph Slatter
James Smith
Sidney Smith
William A. Smith
Gideon Sose
Henry Spencer
Samuel Sprague
William Stephens
Abraham Stevens
Charles B. Stewart
Joseph A. Stovall
Bennett Strunk
Benjamin W. Taliaferro
Memory B. Tatom
Joseph R. Tatom
Kneeland Taylor
George J. W. Thayer
Evans B. Thomas
John Stephen Thorn
Isaac Ticknor
Lewis Tilson

Wilkins S. Turberville
John Tyler
James Vaughan
William E. Vaughan
George Marion Vigal
Frederick J. Volckman
William A. O.
    Wadsworth
William Waggoner
A. J. Wallace
Benjamin C. Wallace
Samuel P. Wallace
William Ward
Nicholas B. Waters
Joseph W. Watson

Alman Weaver
James Webb
James West
Thomas Weston
Ira J. Westover
Orlando Wheeler
James S. Wilder
Henry Wilkey
Abner B. Williams
James Williams
Napoleon B. Williams
Robert W. Wilson
Samuel Wilson
Edward Wingate
James C. Winn

William S. Winningham
Stephen Winship
Andrew Winter
Hughes Witt
Henry H. Wood
John Wood
William P. Wood
Allen Wren
Isaac Newton Wright
Elian Robert Yeamans
Erastus Yeamans
Harrison Young
James O. Young
Solomon Youngblood*

*Historian Harbert Davenport believes that substantial evidence shows that the name Bell Martin should be "Bill Marvin," and Charles J. Carrier, is "Charles J. Carrer"; that Thomas T. Churchill should be "Thomas T. Churchwell"; and John Donoho, "John Donahoo"; that John Kornicky is properly "Isaac Kornicky"; Henry Martin, is "Harvey Martin"; Thomas Reeves, "Thomas Rives"; and Frederick Sevenman, "Frederick Seibenaman."

Escaped From the Goliad Massacre, March 27, 1836:

Thomas G. Allen
William Brenan
Zacharia S. Brooks
Samuel T. Brown
Bennett Butler
Dillard Cooper
Neill John Devenny
John Crettenden Duval
Herman Ehrenberg
William Haddon

Isaac D. Hamilton
Nathaniel Hazen
Joseph W. Hicks
Benjamin H. Holland
John C. Holliday
William L. Hunter
Milton Irish
David J. Jones
Thomas Kemp

William Mason
Daniel Martindale
Daniel Murphy
John Reeves
Charles B. Shain
Augustus V. Sharpe
Wilson Simpson
Sidney Van Bibber
John Williams

Allen, Brown, Ehrenberg, Hamilton, Mason, and Reeves were recaptured after escaping and were held by the Mexicans from a few weeks to many months before escaping again or being released. Devenny, Hamilton, Hunter, and Martindale escaped despite having serious wounds.

Men Spared at Goliad, March 27:

Dr. Joseph H. Barnard
Andrew Michael Boyle
Dr. Joseph E. Field
Francisco Garcia
Peter Griffin
Benjamin H. Hughes

James Hughes
Abel Morgan
George Pittuck
William Rosenburry
William Scurlock

Charles Smith
Joseph H. Spohn
John George Andrew Vose
Alvin E. White
Ulrich Wuthrich

Fannin's Men Not Killed or Captured Because Absent
on March 14-27 Due to Illness or Duty:

John Barton	Joseph Howe	John Smith
Munroe Bullick	Amos D. Jenyon	Simpson Tennant
David N. Burke	Basil Lamar	Francis W. Thornton
Robert Dickinson	John Lowary	John Van Bibber
Francis S. Early	Dr. William H. Magee	Lewis M. H. Washington
Isham J. Good	Bennett McNelly	Joseph T. Williams
Joseph Hopkins	Alexander E. Patton	

Possibly Killed with Colonel Fannin's Command:*

John L. Chambers	Henry L. Ward
Henry H. Eadock	John Ward
Richard Green	

*List compiled using work prepared by Harbert Davenport that appeared in *Southwestern Historical Quarterly*, 48:1-41; John Henry Brown, *The History of Texas*, (St. Louis: Becktold & Co.), 1:622-631.

The Goliad Declaration of Independence, December 20, 1835

. . . That the former province and department of Texas is, and of right ought to be, a free, sovereign and independent State:

> That we hereto set our names, pledge to each other our lives, our fortunes and our sacred honor to sustain this declaration relying with entire confidence upon the cooperation of our fellow-citizens and the approving smiles of the God of the living to aid and conduct us victoriously through the struggle, to the enjoyment of peace, union and good government; and invoking His maledictions if we should either equivocate or, in any manner whatever, prove ourselves unworthy of the high destiny at which we aim.

Signers of the Goliad Declaration of Independence, December 20, 1835, in Goliad Mission:

Miguel Aldrete
Sayle Antonine
J. W. Baylor
J. T. Bell
John Bowen
John J. Bowman
Joseph Bowman
Wm. S. Brown of
    Brazoria
Elkanah Brush
Morgan Bryan
Joseph Cadle
Gustavus Caldwell
M. Carbajal
George W. Cash
J. B. Dale
H. F. Davis
Jeremiah Day
Thomas M. Dennis of
    Matagorda
C. M. Despalier
Andrew Devereau
Philip Dimmitt
Spirse Dooley
James Duncan
John Dunn
James Elder
E.B.W. Fitzgerald
David George
H. George
Wm. Gould
Wm Haddin

Thomas Hanron of
    Matagorda
Timothy Hart
William G. Hill of
    Brazoria
Nathaniel Holbrook
Wm. E. Howeth of
    Brazos
J. C. Hutchins
Peter Hynes
Ira Ingram of Matagorda
John James
John Johnson
D. M. Jones
Francis Jones
Michael Kelly
J. D. Kirkpatrick
Walter Lambert
W. H. Living
Victor Loupy
Alexander Lynch
Charles Malone
Robert McClure
Edward McDonough
Dugald McFarlane of
    Matagorda
Hugh McMinn
Charles Messer
Henry J. Morris
Wm. Newland
Benj. Noble
C. J. O'Connor
James O'Connor

Thomas O'Connor
Michael O'Donnell
Patrick O'Leary
G. W. Paine
C. A. Parker
D. H. Peeks
B. H. Perkins
John Pollan
Lewis Powell
Albert Pratt
Wm. Quinn
Edward Quirk
R.L. Redding
W. Redfield
Wm. Robertson
Isaac Robinson
James W. Scott
Charles Shearn
John Shelly
Albert Silsbee
Francis P. Smith
Horace Stamans
Edward St. John
James St. John
Thomas Todd
Jefferson Ware
George W. Welsh
Allen White
Benj. J. White of
    Navidad
Benj. J. White, Jr.
David Wilson
Alvin Woodward

There were a total of ninety-two signers. Thirty-one were members of one of the Irish colonies that were more exposed to Mexican assault than other colonists. Over one-third of the signers gave their lives for the cause of independence, most as members of Fannin's command.

The declaration was carried to the provisional government at San Felipe by Thomas H. Bell, Benjamin J. White, Sr., William G. Hill, William S. Brown, J. Dodd Kirkpatrick, and John Dunn. The declaration was also printed as a handbill and was printed in a number of papers in the United States as well as in Texas.

The declaration met with a cool reception by the provisional government—they were not yet ready to admit that relations with Mexico were irreparable. It appeared that a majority of the group favored continuing the struggle as a part of Mexico, falling back on the Constitution of 1824. Those speaking up in favor of the declaration were labeled "agitators," "adventurers," and "endangering rights of the old settlers." Continued friendship with the federal party in Mexico was advocated by those opposing the upstart declaration of independence from Goliad. Strangely enough men who leaned toward such a declaration failed to speak out.

There were twenty-one municipalities represented in the Consultation at this time. Those from the Raw Frontier were as follows: Gonzales, J. D. Clements; Brazoria, John A. Wharton, Edwin Waller; Matagorda, R. R. Royall, Charles Wilson, Ira R. Lewis, James Kerr; Victoria, Juan A. Padilla, John J. Linn; Refugio, James Power, John Malone: Goliad, Ira Westover; San Patricio, Lewis Ayers, John McMullen; Jackson, James Kerr (who represented Matagorda until creation of Jackson County in which he lived).[1]

ENDNOTES

Prologue

1. Lewis W. Newton and Herbert P. Gambrell, *A Social and Political History of Texas* (Dallas: Southwest Press, 1932), 12-54; John Hicks, *The Federal Union* (Boston: Houghton Mifflin Co., 1937) 108-109.
2. John Henry Brown, *History of Texas from 1685 to 1892* (St. Louis: L. E. Daniell, 1892), 1:35-44. The survivors were Luciano Garcia, Joseph Reed, David Fero, Solomon Cooley, Jonah Walters, Charles King, Ellis P. Bean, and William Danlin.
3. Walter Prescott Webb et al., *The Handbook of Texas* (Austin: Texas State Historical Association, 1952), 1:255; Brown, *History of Texas*, 1:52-53; Hicks, *The Federal Union*, 275-76.
4. Newton and Gambrell, *History of Texas*, 52-61, 82; Roy Grimes, *300 Years in Victoria County* (Victoria: Victoria Advocate Publishing Co., 1985), 33-35.
5. Brown, *History of Texas*, 64-67; Keith Guthrie, *Texas Forgotten Ports* (Austin: Eakin Press), 2:227, 229.
6. Newton and Gambrell, *History of Texas*, 62; Brown, *History of Texas*, 76-81.
7. Guthrie, *Texas Forgotten Ports*, 2:125. At Jane Long's death in 1880 at eighty-two, the *Galveston News* eulogized her under the headline: "Death of a Texas Heroine."
8. Webb, *The Handbook of Texas*, 1:643; David J. Weber, *Foreigners in Their Native Land* (Albuquerque: University of New Mexico Press, 1976), 90.
9. Guthrie, *Texas Forgotten Ports*, 1:119.
10. Webb, *The Handbook of Texas*, 1:745.
11. Alleine Howren, "Causes and Origin of the Decree of April 6, 1830" *Southwest Historical Quarterly*, 16:415.

Chapter 1. Spanish Land Grants

1. Quotation from Jonathan Edwards, "Freedom of the Will," 1754.
2. Webb, *The Handbook*, 1:256.
3. John E. Rouse, *The Cariollo, Spanish Cattle in the Americas* (Norman: University of Oklahoma Press, 1977), 33.
4. Webb, *The Handbook*, 1:571.
5. D. E. Kilgore, *Nueces County, Texas 1750-1800, A Bicentennial Memoir* (Corpus Christi: Friends of the Corpus Christi Museum, 1975), 4, 5.
6. Nell White, *Goliad in the Texas Revolution* (Privately printed in 1988 by Nell White Hargreaves), 7. Book was based on Miss White's master's thesis at the University of Houston in 1941.
7. Robert H. Thonhoff, *El Fuerte Del Cibolo. Sentinel of the Bexar-La Bahia Ranches* (Austin: Eakin Press, 1992), 26-27.
8. Ibid., 37.
9. Ibid., 38.
10. Ibid., 32-35.
11. *Bee Picayane*, "Memories of Old Bee County, History of Casa Blanca," by Camp Ezell (reprinted from an article in the *San Antonio Express*, December 13, 1931. The series ran for five weeks in May of 1950).
12. Series of articles by John Norris, confidant of Mrs. Wallis Wade for over thirty years, that appeared in the *Mathis News* in July and August of 1985. Mrs. Wade died in 1973. The abstract is now in the John Connor Museum, Kingsville, Texas.
13. Charles Deaton, *Texas Postal History Handbook* (Privately printed, 1991), 82.
14. *Bee Picayune*, second installment.
15. Taylor, Paul Schuster, *An American-Mexican Frontier, Nueces County, Texas* (New York: Russell & Russell, 1934), 320-21.
16. D. E. Kilgore, "Spanish and Mexican Land Grants," paper prepared after authoring *Nueces County, Texas 1700-1800, A Bicentennial Memoir* (Corpus Christi: Friends of the Corpus Christi Museum, December 1975), (Mr. Kilgore, a certified public accountant, was a noted historian, having authored a number of books and historical papers. He was also an authority on Sally Scull.)
17. J. Frank Dobie, *Coronado's Children* (Austin: University of Texas Press, 1981), 84-88. Todd McNeill is reported to have dug up $40,000 in money buried in the Ramirez home. His reputation included killing two or three white men and no telling how many Mexicans. When asked to show his land abstract he pointed to his .44 Winchester and commented: "Nobody ain't ever questioned the abstract yet."

18. Dudley Dobie, "Lagarto Near Vanishing Point . . .," *San Antonio Express*, November 18, 1934.

Chapter 2. Start of Armed Conflict

1. Mary Delaney Boddie, *Thunder on the Brazos* (Dallas: Taylor Publishing Co., 1978), 15-22. The trouble at Velasco grew out of discontent over the establishment of Anahuac as a customs house in 1821 and the assignment of Juan Davis Bradburn to the post in 1830 to carry out the provisions of the Law of April 6, 1830. Citizens in the area became incised when Mexican officials moved to abolish the *ayuntamiento* at Liberty and move all affairs to Anahuac where the military would have control over all civil matters. The arrest of Patrick C. Jank and William B. Travis caused a demand by angry settlers for their release. Bradburn was relieved of his command and the garrison was recalled. Walter Prescott Webb and H. Bailey Carroll, eds., *The Handbook of Texas* (Austin: the Texas State Historical Association, 1952), 1:43; Margaret Swett Henson, Juan Davis Bradburn, (College Station: Texas A&M University Press, 1982), 75-80.

2. John Henry Brown, *History of Texas, from 1685 to 1892* (St. Louis: L. E. Daniell, 1892), 1:176.

3. Brown, *History of Texas*, 1:190; Webb, ed., *The Handbook of Texas* 1:388, 404, 479, 2:81, 836; James David Carter, *Education and Masonry in Texas to 1846* (Waco: Grand Lodge of Texas, A.F. and A.M., 1963), 44, 45, 48; Keith Guthrie, *Texas Forgotten Ports*, (Austin: Eakin Press, 1993), 2:105-6. Branch T. Archer was identified with the War Party principally due to his call for immediate independence for Texas. He participated in the Battle of Gonzales but left to attend the Consultation and, as president, he sought to steer a neutral course. He was named as a commissioner, together with Stephen F. Austin and William H. Wharton, to the United States to promote support and raise money. He served in the first Texas Congress and was elected speaker of the House of Representatives in its second term.

4. Eugene C. Barker, ed., *The Austin Papers* (Austin: The University of Texas, 1926), 3:144, 2:151; Webb, *Handbook*, 1:738, 2:52. Gonzales cannon note: No one seems to know just how the cannon got "lost" but somehow or other the Gonzales cannon disappeared. Dr. Patrick J. Wagner of Shiner came across the old cannon in San Antonio in a Texas arms exhibit of the National Rifle Association show. It was owned by Henry Guerra and was not for sale. The Shiner doctor almost forgot the old cannon until he spotted it again, this time in the Texas Gun Collector's Association show. Again it was not for sale, but finally the doctor, who was a collector of renown, traded an undis-

closed amount of rare coins for the Gonzales cannon. The full saga of how the Gonzales cannon was finally proved to be authentic can be found in: Jane Bradfield, *Rx Take One Cannon* (Shiner: Patrick J. Wagner Research and Publishing Co., 1981).

5. Lewis W. Newton and Herbert P. Gambrell, *A Social and Political History of Texas* (Dallas: Southwest Press, 1932), 152; Ethel Zivley Rather, "DeWitt's Colony," *Southwestern Historical Quarterly*, 8:146-151; Frederick Dixon Kemp, "A History of Gonzales County in the Nineteenth Century," Master of Arts Thesis, (Austin: University of Texas, 1964), 3; Vertical file, Gonzales Public Library: "Gonzales Was Featured by Progressive Farmer," *Progressive Farmer*, 1953; "Outstanding Dates in DeWitt's Colony," *Gonzales Inquirer*; "Gonzales, the Lexington of Texas," Barker, *Austin Papers*, 3:146.

6. *Houston Telegraph and Register*, Saturday, October, 1835 (Published in San Felipe); "DeWitt's Colony," *Southwestern Historical Quarterly*, 8-151-156; Barker, *Austin Papers*, 3:146.

7. Barker, *Austin Papers*, 3:147-150, 152-153, 155, 160; Hobart Huson, *Refugio, A Comprehensive History of Refugio County From Aboriginal Times to 1953* (Houston: Guardsman Publishing Co., 1953), 1:212.

8. Brown, *History of Texas from 1685 to 1892*, 1:307-9; Huson, *Refugio*, 2:194; Louis J. Wortham, *A History of Texas From Wilderness to Commonwealth* (Fort Worth: Wortham-Molyneaux Co.), 2:194; Webb, *Handbook of Texas*, 1:326.

9. Huson, *Refugio*, 1:211-15; Huson, *Captain Philip Dimmitt's Commandancy of Goliad, 1835-1836* (Austin: Von Boeckmann-Jones Co., 1974), 6; John J. Linn, *Reminiscences of Fifty Years in Texas* (Austin: State House Press, 1986), 40, 106, 107; Brown, *History of Texas*, 303-4.

10. Barker, *Austin Papers*, 3:68, 131, 137, 142, 164, 189; Guthrie, *Texas Forgotten Ports*), 129, 130; Huson, *Refugio*, 1:217; Frank W. Johnson, Eugene C. Barker and Ernest William Winkler, *A History of Texas and Texans* (Chicago and New York: American Historical Society 1960, 1:176-77. Ben Milam, a veteran of the War of 1812 and a trader with the Comanche Indians in Texas as early as 1818, was also a soldier of fortune taking part in Dr. James Long's failed venture. It is ironic that on October 8, 1821, Milam was with Long when they captured Goliad. Later he became a citizen of Mexico, secured an *impresario* grant of his own, but worked with Arthur G. Wavell in getting colonists for the Wavel *empresario* grant on the Red River. In 1835 he was taken prisoner by a squad under General Perfecto de Cos and taken to Mexico, escaping in time to join Collinsworth's attack on Goliad. He inspired Texans to follow him in the successful assault on Bexar, but was killed by a rifle ball just minutes before the victory. A

monument to him was erected in 1897 by the De Zavala chapter of Daughters of Republic of Texas near the Veramendi House in San Antonio. *Southwestern Historical Quarterly*, Vol. 38; Webb, *Handbook of Texas*, 2:191; Henry Stuart Foote, *Texas and the Texans* (Philadelphia: Thomas Cowperthwait & Co., 1841), 118.

11. Lack, Paul D., *The Texas Revolutionary Experience* (College Station: Texas A&M University Press, 1992), 183.

12. Huson, *Dimmitt's Commandancy*, 18, 19; Barker, *The Austin Papers*, 3:189-90.

13. "Order to Smith et al.," October 12, 1835, Austin's *Order Book*, Q, 4. Lists of men who served during the taking of La Bahia, as well as those who served under Captain Dimmitt, will be found in the appendices in the back of the book.

14. William H. Oberste, *Remember Goliad* (Austin: Von Boeckman-Jones, 1949), 53-54; Hobart Huson, *Captain Philip Dimmitt's* Chapter 1.

15. Barker, *Austin Papers*, 3:176.

16. Bexar Archives (Texas A&M-Corpus Christi University library) Angel Navarto to alcalde of Goliad, Sept. 21, 1835, reel 166, frame 808; Memorial/Petitions (San Patricio seeking permission to operate under pre-revolution framework) Texas State Archives.

17. Barker, *Austin Papers*, 3:213-214; Dimmitt is thought to have seen the Brown flag (Captain William S. Brown designed a flag while at the siege of Bexar) and designed his own along similar lines. Miss Mary A. Mitchell (*First Flag of Texas Independence*, 18, 19) believes the Goliad flag had a field of white, upon which the red and bloody arm and sword was emblazoned without any lettering. Mamie Wynne Cox (*The Romantic Flags of Texas*, 180-81) says the flag had the word "Independence" across the third white stripe from the top. Brown was actually a member of the Dimmitt command in December of 1835. He is supposed to have taken his flag with him to Velasco where it was displayed. Dimmitt's flag remained flying at Goliad, at least until January 6, 1836, when Dr. James Grant entered the presidio with his force and threatened to tear the flag down, after which Dimmitt lowered the flag to forestall a confrontation. (*Captain Phillip Dimmitt's Commandaancy of Goliad, 1835-36*, 239).

18. *Jenkins Papers*, 3:51; Guthrie, *Texas Forgotten Ports*, 2:105-107. A group of citizens, headed by Henry Smith and John Austin, gathered in Brazoria to get a cannon to use against Mexican forces at Anahuac. Over 100 men were gathered and after much planning they enlisted John G. Rowland, master of the riverboat *Brazoria* to make a run down the river, past Fort Velasco held by Mexican forces

commanded by Col. Domingo de Ugartechea. Attacked by land and from the Brazoria the Mexicans surrendered the fort to the Texans. The Texans lost seven killed and fourteen wounded, three dying later. The Mexicans had five killed and sixteen wounded. Blood had been spilled!

19. Rachel Bluntzer Hebert, *The Forgotten Colony* (Burnet: Eakin Press, 1981), 200-201; Huson, *Refugio*, 1:126.

20. Clarence R. Wharton, *Texas, Under Many Flags*, (Chicago/New York: American Historical Society), 12:181-188; Huson, *Refugio*, 1:144-145; Guthrie, Keith, *History of San Patricio County*, (Austin: Nortex Publishers, 1986), 12, 13; John J. Linn, *Reminiscences of Fifty Years in Texas*, (Austin: State House Press, 1986), 119; "Archeological Investigations at Fort Lipantitlan," December 1988, by James E. Warren with Skip Kennedy and Nancy Beaman (earlier report was done in 1974 by J. Daviding, Archeological Report 16, Texas Parks and Wildlife Department); Webb, *Handbook of Texas*, 2:190.

21. John H. Jenkins, ed., *The Papers of the Texas Revolution, 1835-1836* (Austin: Presidial Press, 1973), 8:194-196.

22. Linn, *Fifty Years in Texas*, 119.

23. Linn, *Fifty Years in Texas*, 118-122; Huson, *Refugio*, 226-230; Huson, *Dimmitt*, 98-104; Guthrie, *History of San Patricio County*, 12-13; Hebert, *The Forgotten Colony*, 36-40; Jenkins Papers, 2:275-277, 384-385, 431-432, 3:51.

24. William Campbell Binkley, *The Expansionist Movement in Texas, 1836-1850* (Berkeley: University of California Press, 1925) 1:86-87; Huson, *Dimmitt*, 108, 109.

25. Eugene Barker, *Writings of Sam Houston 1813-1863*, (Austin: The University of Texas Press, 1938), 1:307.

26. Brown, *History of Texas*, 1:375-379; Huson, *Refugio*, 1:233-234; *Austin Papers*, 3:248-251, 258-260; "Austin's Order Book," *Southwestern Historical Quarterly*, 11:47, 48.

27. Brown, *History of Texas*, 1:377-379; Huson, *Refugio*, 1:238; Proceedings of the General Council, 147, 187-188; *Gamel Laws of Texas*, 1:715, 735-736, 756. Dimmitt's flag was also called the Brown flag. A committee made up of John Dunn, William S. Brown, Thomas H. Baell, Benjamin J. White, Sr., and William G. Hill was appointed to carry the declaration to the General Council meeting at San Felipe. A list of the signers of the Goliad Declaration of Independence will be found in the appendices.

28. Huson, *Refugio*, 239; Brown, *History of Texas*, 1:432, 503; Proceedings of the General Council, 147, 187-188, 208; *Lamar Papers*, 5:368.

29. Williams and Barker, *Writings of Sam Houston*, 1:326, 328, 379.

30. Harbert Davenport, "The Men of Goliad," *Southwestern Historical Quarterly*, 43:5-10; Huson, *Refugio*, 1:259ff; Hebert, *The Forgotten Colony*, 44-45, 83-91, 93-94; *Lamar Papers*, 1:272-73, 5:375; *Austin Papers*, 2:50-51. 2:320; H. Yoakum, *History of Texas* (New York: Redfield, 1856), 2:426; H.P.N. Gammel, ed., *Laws of Texas 1822-1897* (Austin: The Gammel Book Co., 1898) , 460-470; Brown, *History of Texas*, 1:517; Wharton, *Remember Goliad*, 35.

Chapter 3. Texas Political Realities in 1835-36

1. Brown, *History of Texas*, 1:383-385, 542, 558-559, 564, 587; Webb, *Handbook of Texas*, 1:84, 677, 678; John Henry Brown, *Life and Times of Henry Smith* (Austin: Steck Co., 1935), 97, 162, 208, 209, 213.
2. John Henry Brown, *History of Texas from 1685 to 1892* (St. Louis: L. E. Daniell, 1892), 1:542, 558-559, 564, 587; Webb, *The Handbook of Texas* 1:84, 677-78; John Henry Brown, *Life and Times of Henry Smith* (Austin: Steck Co., 1935), 97, 162, 208, 209, 213; H.P.N. Gammel, *The Laws of Texas, 1822-1897* (Austin: The Gammel Book Company, 1898), 1:211, 214.
3. John Henry Brown, *History of Texas From 1685 to 1892* (St. Louis: L. E. Daniell Publishers, 1892), 1:608-09; Jose Enrique de la Pena, *With Santa Anna in Texas* (College Station: Texas A&M University Press, 1975), 78; Carlos E. Castaneda, *The Mexican side of the Texan Revolution* (Austin: Graphic Ideas, Inc. 1970), 19, 108-09.
4. Pena, *With Santa Anna in Texas*, 70.
5. Castaneda, *The Mexican Side of the Texan Revolution*, 228.
6. Ed Kilman, *Cannibal Coast* (San Antonio: The Naylor Company, 1959), 249-53.
7. Pena, *With Santa Anna in Texas*, 68, 69.
8. Ibid., 70.
9. Hobart Huson, *Captain Philip Dimmitt's Commandancy of Goliad, 1835-1836*, Austin: Von Boeckmann-Jones Co., 1974), 83.
10. *Lucio Moya, et al. vs O'Connor, Estate of J. M. O'Brien and Nannie Hart O'Brien, 36th Judicial District, Bee County*, May 16, 1975, No. 13:758.
11. Hobart Huson, *Refugio, A Comprehensive History of Refugio County*, (Houston: The Guardsman Publishing Co., 1953), 1:221-22.
12. Huson, *Dimmitt's Commandancy*, 118-123.
13. Stephen F. Austin, *Austin Papers*, (Austin: University of Texas Press, 1927), 3:246; Huson, *Refugio*, 233-34.
14. "S. F. Austin to Jose Maria Gonzales, Nov. 18, 1835," John H. Jenkins,

The Papers of the Texas Revolution, (Austin: Presidial Press, 1973), 2:450; "J. W. Fannin, Jr. to Stephen F. Austin, Nov. 18, 1835," 2:457; Brown, *History of Texas*, 1:373, 374.

15. Paul D. Lack, *The Texas Revolutionary Experience*, (College Station: Texas A&M University Press, 1992, 165, 186, 187; "Stephen F. Austin to Jose Maria Gonzales, Nov. 18, 1835," Jenkins, *The Papers of the Texas Revolution*, 2:450.

16. "Austin's Proclamation to the Inhabitants of Bexar," Jenkins, *The Papers of the Texas Revolution*, 2:252-54.

17. "Bowie and Fannin to Austin, Oct. 22, 23, 1835," Jenkins, *The Papers of the Texas Revolution*, 2:190-91, 202-203; "Austin to Antonio de la Garza, Nov. 16, 1835," Jenkins, *The Papers of the Texas Revolution*, 2:433.

18. Rachel Bluntzer Hebert, *The Forgotten Colony, San Patricio de Hibernia*, (Burnet: Eakin Press, 1981), 26.

19. Hebert, *The Forgotten Colony*, 1, 24, 64, 124.

20. Harriet Smither, editor, *The Papers of Mirabeau Buonaparte Lamar*, (Austin: Von Boeckmann-Jones Co.), 5:85, 88.

21. Jenkins, *The Papers of the Texas Revolution*, 2:69, 73-74.

22. Huson, *Dimmitt's Commandancy*, 102; *Houston Telegraph and Register*, December 2, 1835; John J. Linn, *Reminiscences of Fifty Years in Texas*, (Austin: State House Press, 1886), 120-21. Linn was a personal friend of Lieutenant Garcia and one of the lieutenant's last words was to give his fine horse to Linn. There is no record of a surgeon living in San Patricio; however, through her research Rachal Bluntzer Hebert found that the doctor could have been James Cullen, M.D.

23. Eugene C. Barker, ed., *The Austin Papers*, (Austin: The University of Texas Press, 1926), 3:208; Jenkins, *The Papers of the Texas Revolution*, 2:146.

24. "John J. Linn to Austin," Goliad, Oct. 17, 1835, *Austin Papers*, 2:189-90.

25. Jenkins, *Papers of the Texas Revolution*, 3:76.

26. San Patricio County census of 1850.

27. Hebert, *Forgotten Colony*, 126-27, 183-84.

28. H.P.N. Gammel, *The Laws of Texas 1822-1897*, (Austin: The Gammel Book Co., 1898), 1:656; Texas State Historical Association, "McGloin to Ayers," 9:227.

Chapter 4. Volunteers Gather at Gonzales

1. John Henry Brown, *A History of Texas 1685 to 1892* (St. Louis: L. E. Daniell 1892), 1:309-310, 366, 367; Hobart Huson, *Refugio: A Com-*

prehensive History of Refugio County from Aboriginal Times to 1953 (Houston: The Guardsman Publishing Co., 1953), 1:215.

2. William T. Austin, *A Comprehensive History of Texas*, 1:538-540; Ethel Zebley Rather, "Dewitt's Colony," *Southwestern Historical Quarterly*, 8:157-58; *Houston Telegraph and Register*, Saturday, October 1835; Eugene C. Barker et al., eds., *The Austin Papers* (Austin: The University of Texas Press), 3:150.

3. Walter P. Webb et al., eds., *The Handbook of Texas* (Austin: State Historical Association, 1952), 1:84; Louis J. Wortham, *A History of Texas from Wilderness to Commonwealth*, (Fort Worth: Wortham-Molyneaux Co., 1924), 2:356-57.

4. Eugene Barker, *Austin Papers* (Austin: University of Texas Press, 1927), 3:212.

5. Barker, *Austin Papers*, "Whilliam H. Jack to Austin," Goliad, October 13, 1835, 3:178; "R. R. Royal to Austin," San Felipe, October 13, 1835, 3:178; "Benjamin Fort Smith to Austin," Goliad, October 1835, 3:182-83; "Phillip Dimmitt to Austin," October 20, 1835, 3:194-195.

6. Brown, *A History of Texas*, 1:369-371.

7. Richardson, (Richard or R. R.) Royal was born in Halifax County, Virginia, in 1798 and came to Texas with eleven prominent families from Tuscumbia, Alabama, as a member of Stephen F. Austin's colony and established a plantation in Matagorda in 1832. Active in the affairs of the colony, he was president of the committee of safety of Matagorda municipality, delegate to the Convention of 1833, temporary chairman of Consultation of 1835, and a member of the General Council of the provisional government. When Stephen F. Austin left to take command of the Texas army he was elected to take Austin's place as president on October 11, 1835. From October 11 to 31 the Permanent Council was the government of Texas. All business was done in the name of the Permanent Council of Texas. He joined McCoy's Company, a group of mounted riflemen, in April of 1836 and later was authorized by President David Burnet to raise an independent ranger company to round up ownerless cattle to use as food for the Texas Army. He was a merchant and gin owner. He died May 28, 1840, and is buried in Matagorda Cemetery. Source: *Historic Matagorda County* (Houston: D. Armstrong Co., Inc., 1986), 1:88.

8. Wortham, *History of Texas*, 2:369.

9. Brown, *History of Texas*, 1:719.

10 Webb et al., eds., *The Handbook of Texas*, 719.

11. Wortham, *A History of Texas*, 3:51-52; Harbert Davenport, "Captain Jesus Cuellar, Texas Cavalry, Otherwise Comanche." *Southwestern Historical Quarterly*, 48:56-62. Ben Milam was a soldier of fortune, an adventurer, and a true Texas patriot. He was a participant in the War

of 1812 and soon thereafter was engaged in a venture to take a ship
loaded with flour from New Orleans to South America. The crew
came down with yellow fever, but Milam was rescued after a ship-
wreck. He showed up trading with the Comanche Indians at the head
of the Colorado River in 1818. Later he became involved with Dr.
James Long, and after this failure, joined the Mexican army, applied
for citizenship and sought an *empresario* grant in Texas. In 1831 he
was successful in getting a small steamer past the Red River raft to the
proposed Wavell's Red River grant. Following up on this project, he
was in Monclova in 1835 seeking titles to the Red River land. He was
taken prisoner by soldiers under General Perfecto de Cos, escaped and
joined Collinsworth's force the night they stormed La Bahia. He lost
his life in the Battle of Bexar. For years he had been on the cutting
edge of change in the future state of Texas. Source: Webb et al., eds.,
The Handbook of Texas, 1:191.
12. Wortham, *A History of Texas*, 54-62.
13. Webb, *The Handbook of Texas*, 1:154.

Chapter 5. The Matamoros Expedition

1. Hobart Huson, *Refugio: a Comprehensive History of Refugio County from Aboriginal Times to 1953* (Houston: Guardsman Publishing Co.1953), 1:261; Frank W. Johnson, *Texas and Texans* (Chicago and New York: The American Historical Society, 1914), 1:419-427.
2. Eugene C. Barker, ed., *The Austin Papers* (Austin: The University of Texas, 1926), 3:253.
3. Louis J. Wortham, *History of Texas* (Fort Worth: Wortham Molyneaux Company, 1924), 54-62.
4. Huson, *Refugio*, 1:262.
5. Amelia Williams and Eugene Barker, eds., *The Writings of Sam Houston*, (Austin: University of Texas Press, 1943), 1:322-323, 328-329.
6. H.P.N. Gammel, *The Laws of Texas, 1822-1897*, (Austin: The Gammel Book Company, 1898), 1:746; Huson, *Refugio*, 1:261. In a letter to Governor Henry Smith on January 10, 1836, Houston said: "I am told that Frank Johnson and Fannin have obtained from the Military Committee orders to proceed and reduce Matamoros. It may not be so. There was no Quorum, and the Council could not give power." Williams and Barker, eds, *The Writings of Sam Houston*, 1:334.
7. Williams and Barker, eds., *The Writings of Sam Houston*, 1:341-342, 352, 353. The Tampico Expedition, led by George Fisher and Jose Antonio Mexia, left New Orleans November 5, 1835, with 150 men

on the schooner *Mary Jane* to advance the cause of Federalism. The schooner went aground, and a premature uprising of the garrison on November 13, doomed the American attack, leaving behind thirty-three men as prisoners; of these, three died of wounds and the others were tried and shot on December 14. Source: Walter P. Webb et al., eds., *The Handbook of Texas*, (Austin: The Texas State Historical Association, 1952), 2:704-705.

8. Ibid., 340 note 8, 352.

9. Ibid., 405-6.

10. Ibid., 515-16.

11. Walter P. Webb et al., eds., *The Handbook of Texas*, (Austin: The State Historical Association, 1952), 1:582.

12. John H. Jenkins, *Papers of the Texas Revolution*, (Austin: Presidial Press, 1973), 3:324.

13. Ibid., 325.

14. Harriet Smither, ed., *The Papers of Mirabeau Buonaparte Lamar* (Austin: Von Boeckmann-Jones Co., 1927), 5:380; Hobart Huson, *Captain Phillip Dimmitt's Commandancy of Goliad* (Austin: Von Boeckmann-Jones Co., 1974), 228-29; William Campbell Binkley, *Official Correspondence of the Texas Revolution, 1835-1836* (New York: D. Appleton-Century Co., 1936), 1:784-85.

15. *Lamar Papers*, 5:380-81.

16. Rachel Bluntzer Hebert, *The Forgotten Colony*, (Burnet: Eakin Press, 1981), 89; Webb, *The Handbook of Texas*, 2:673. Stillman was the founder of Brownsville and one of the men who developed steamboat traffic on the Rio Grande to bring supplies up the river to General Zachary Taylor during and after the Mexican War.

17. Frank W. Johnson, *A History of Texas and Texans*, (Chicago: The American History Society, 1916), 420.

18. James McGloin, "Historical Notes," *Lamar Papers*, 5:380-383; Johnson, *Texas and Texans*, 419-422.

19. Jose Enrique de la Pena, *With Santa Anna in Texas*, (College Station: Texas A&M University Press), 68, 69; Carlos E. Castaneda, *The Mexican Side of the Texan Revolution*, (Dallas: Graphic Ideas, Inc.), 11, 12, 13: *Lamar Papers*, 5:382.

20. Castaneda, *Mexican Side of the Texan Revolution*, 214-218; Keith Guthrie, *History of San Patricio County*, (Austin: Eakin Press, 1986), 13; Pena, *With Santa Anna in Texas*, 68, 69; Harbart Davenport, "The Men of Goliad!" *The Southwestern Historical Quarterly*, 48:28, 29, (July, 1939). A list of Johnson's and Grant's men will be found in the appendices.

Chapter 6. Goliad/Refugio Campaigns

1. Lucian Knight Laour, *Georgia's Bi-Centennial Memoirs and Memories*, (Privately printed by author and dedicated to Hon. Cordell Hull, a friend of the author, 1933), 278; "Letter of James W. Fannin to Major Belton," August 27, 1835, *Southwestern Historical Quarterly*, April 1904, 7:318, "Letter: '. . . We will be glad to see as many West Point boys as can be spared—Many of whom are known to me & by whom I am known as J. W. Walker—My maternal Grandfather's name, & by whom I was raised and adopted & whose name I then bore'"; Clarence Wharton, *Remember Goliad* (Glorieta, N.M.: The Rio Grande Press, Inc., 1931), 1; Letter of Librarian Edward S. Holden, of U.S. Military Academy, to Dr. C. W. Raines, State Librarian, Austin, Texas *Southwestern Historical Quarterly*, 7:320; Nell White, *Goliad in the Texas Revolution* (Privately printed in 1988 by Nell White Hargreaves). Based on thesis presented to Graduate School, University of Houston for Master of Arts, 1941, 29.

2. Keith Guthrie, *Texas Forgotten Ports*, (Austin: Eakin Publishing Co., 1993), 2:121; James David Carter, *Masonry in Texas*, 267.

3. John Henry Brown, *History of Texas* (St. Louis: L.E. Daniell, 1992), 1:472-479; Walter P. Webb et al., eds., *The Handbook of Texas* (Austin: The Texas State Historical Association, 1952), 1:582; Eugene C. Barker and Amelia W. Williams, eds., *The Writings of Sam Houston* (Austin: The University of Texas Press, 1938), "Houston to J. W. Fannin, San Felipe, Nov. 13, 1835," 1:305, Houston to James W. Robinson, January 11, 1836, 1:334, (Houston pointed out that the council lacked a quorum, making the authorization illegal.); Wharton, *Remember Goliad*, 36.

4. William C. Binkley, *The Expansionist Movement in Texas, 1836-1870* (Berkley: University of California Publications in History, 1925), "Robinson to Tarlton, et al.," February 7, 1836, 1:365-366; Hobart Huson, *Refugio, A Comprehensive History of Refugio County From Aboriginal Times to 1953* (Houston: Guardsman Publishing Co., 1953), 1:275-279. Huson pointed out that Fannin had erred when he spoke of lack of support from the colonists since Westover's company was composed of local Irishmen and Fraser's Refugio militia had over twenty-five local men. Harbert Davenport, "The Men of Goliad," *Southwestern Historical Quarterly*, 48:12-13; Webb, *The Handbook of Texas*, 2:453. The importance of Copano was emphasized again and again. Houston sent Col. Peyton S. Wyatt with two attachments of auxiliary volunteers to Copano for protection on December 28, 1835, *Writings of Sam Houston*, 1:326.

5. *Houston Telegraph and Register*, January 9, 1836. In this same issue mail route No. 10 from Victoria, by Goliad and Refugio, to San Patricio, one hundred miles, once in two weeks was advertised; Huson, *Refugio*, 1:275; Brown, *History of Texas*, 1:475.
6. Huson, *Refugio*, 1:277-79; Wharton, *Remember Goliad*, 36.
7. Huson, *Refugio*, 1:272.
8. Henry Stuart Foote, *Texas and the Texans* (Philadelphia: Thomas, Cowperthwait & Co., 1841), 224-27. Bower came to Texas in the fall of 1835 and, as a representative of San Patricio to the Convention of 1836, was a signer of the declaration of independence.
9. "Houston to James Collinsworth, March 13, 1836," *Writings of Sam Houston*, 1:367.
10. Harbert Davenport, "Captain Jesus Cuellar," *Southwestern Historical Quarterly*, 30:56-62; Carlos E. Castaneda, *The Mexican Side of the Texan Revolution*, (Austin/Dallas: Graphic Ideas, Inc., 1970), 216-17; General Vincente Filisola, translated by Wallace Woolsey, *The History of the War in Texas* (Austin: Eakin Press, 1983), 2:190-91.
11. Huson, *Refugio*, 1:284; Davenport, "Men of Goliad," *Southwestern Historical Quarterly*, 48:20-21.
12. Frank W. Johnson, *A History of Texas and Texans* (Chicago: The American Historical Society, 1916), 1:423. (An eyewitness account written by survivor R. R. Brown). Huson, *Refugio*, 1:289; Louis J. Wortham, *History of Texas from Wilderness to Commonwealth* (Fort Worth: Wortham-Molyneaux Company, 1924), 3:174.
13. Wharton, *Remember Goliad*, 39; Foote, *Texas and the Texans*, Letter of James W. Fannin to the government, February 28, 1836, 2:225.
14. *Lamar Papers*, 1:136; *Writings of Sam Houston*, 1:367; Johnson, *Texas and Texans*, 2:216.
15. Huson, *Refugio*, 1:287-88; *Lamar Papers*, 1:334.
16. Davenport, "Men of Goliad," *Southwestern Historical Quarterly*, 48:23; Huson, *Refugio*, 1:287-88..
17. Huson, *Refugio*, 1:293-94; Foote, *Lamar Papers*, 1:337.
18. Foote, *History of Texas*, 2:255-56.
19. Huson, *Refugio*, 1:295; Foote, *History of Texas*, 2:255; *Lamar Papers*, 2:10-12.
20. *Lamar papers*, 2:11; Huson, *Refugio*, 1:296-297; Davenport, "Men of Goliad," *Southwestern Historical Quarterly*, 48:23.
21. Davenport, "Men of Goliad," *Southwestern Historical Quarterly*, 48:31; Huson, *Refugio*, 1:296.
22. "Ayers Account," *Southwestern Historical Quarterly*, 9:274; Huson, *Refugio*, 1:309-314.

23. *Lamar Papers*, 5:375; "Houston to James W. Fannin," *Writings of Sam Houston*, Headquarters, Gonzales, March 11, 1836, 1:364.

24. *Lamar Papers*, 2:10-12; Dr. J. H. Barnard's Journal, Printed by *Goliad Advance*. The journal was first published in the Goliad Guard's office in 1883 and reprinted in 1912 by the *Goliad Advance*, J. A. White, ed., 15.

25. *Lamar Papers*, 4:239-40; Castaneda, *Mexican Side of the Texas Revolution*, 220; *Writings of Houston*, 1:362-63.

26. Huson, *Refugio*, 1:309-11; Castaneda, *The Mexican Side of the Texan Revolution*, 219-221; Refugio Timely Remarks, May 11, 1934, June 15, 1934, June 22, 1934.

27. Huson, *Refugio*, 1:214, 221-22, 288, 293-94, 301, 310-11, 320-21, 365, 370, 411-12; Davenport, "The Men of Goliad," *Southwestern Historical Quarterly*, 43:11, 31; *Lamar Papers*,1:336; Barnard's Journal, 11.

28. Wortham, *A History of Texas from Wilderness to Commonwealth*, 3:117-134. This long dispatch from Houston, addressed to Governor Smith, lays out Houston's problems with the General Council and other military commanders.

29. Wortham, *History of Texas*, 3:171.

30. *Writings of Sam Houston*, 7:311; Castaneda, *Mexican Side of the Texas Revolution*, 221.

31. Don Vicente Filisola, translated by Wallace Woolsey, *Memoirs for the History of the War in Texas*, (Austin: Eakin Press, 1987), 2:197-198. Filisola says that Urrea had about 200 troops; however, in Urrea's *Diario* the general said that he left Refugio with 900 men. Actually, Historian Hobart Huson estimated that he had at least 1,400 troops at his disposal to deal with Fannin's 302 men; Carlos E. Castaneda, *The Mexican Side of the Texan Revolution*, (Dallas: P.L. Turner Company, 1935), 221; Hobart Huson, *A Comprehensive History of Refugio County From Aboriginal Times to 1953*, (Houston: The Guardsman Publishing Co., 1953), 312.

32. James Collinsworth was chairman of the Military Committee of the General Council, signer of the declaration of independence and introduced the resolution to make Sam Houston commander in chief of the Texas Army for the second time. He participated in the Battle of San Jacinto and in the affairs of the new Republic. He was elected a senator from the Brazoria District and then as chief justice of the Supreme Court of Texas. He became a candidate for presidency of the Republic but committed suicide by drowning in Galveston Bay. (*The Writings of Sam Houston*, 1:369 footnote).

33. Nell White, *Goliad in the Texas Revolution*, (privately printed by Nell White Hargreaves, 1941), 41.

34. John Henry Brown, *History of Texas From 1685 to 1892*, (St. Louis: L. E. Daniell, 1892), 1:594.
35. Dr. J. H. Barnard, *Barnard's Journal* (Goliad: *Goliad Advance*, 1912, reprinted 1965), 14-16: Henry Stuart Foote, *Texas and the Texans*, Philadelphia: Thomas, Cowperthwait & Co.), 2:229; Clarence Wharton, *Remember Goliad*, (Glorieta, N.M.: The Rio Grande Press, Inc., 1931), 40; Harbert Davenport, "The Men of Goliad," *Southwestern Historical Quarterly*, 48:24.
36. Huson, *Refugio*, 1:324-325; White, *Goliad in the Texas Revolution*, 42-43.
37. Brown, *History of Texas*, 594.
38. Huson, *Refugio*, 1:326; White, *Goliad in the Texas Revolution*, 43; William Kennedy, *Texas, Its Geography, Natural History and Topography* (New York: Benjamin & Young, 1844), 1:567; Barnard, *Barnard's Journal*, 16.
39. SNAFU is slang for "Situation all fouled up"; Barnard, *Barnard's Journal*, 17.
40. Davenport, "Men of Goliad," *Southwest Historical Quarterly*, 48:43; Huson, *Refugio*, 328-329; Brown, *History of Texas*, 601.
41. Barnard, *Barnard's Journal*, 17. Ironically Ehrenburg was later one of the men who escaped the massacre; John C. Duval, edited by Mabel Major and Rebecca W. Smith, *Early Times in Texas*, (Lincoln: University of Nebraska Press, 1986), 63; Castaneda, *The Mexican Side of Texan Revolution*, 223.
42. Foote, *Texas and the Texans*, 2:232.
43. Huson, *Refugio*, 1:332; Barnard, *Barnard's Journal*, 18.
44. Barnard, *Barnard's Journal*, 18-19; Davenport, *Southwest Historical Quarterly*, 4:8-17; Huson, *Refugio*, 1:335.
45. Huson, *Refugio*, 1:334.
46. Duval, *Early Times in Texas*, 69; White, *Goliad in the Texas Revolution*, 44. Henry D. Ripley is listed as having been killed at the massacre on March 27, 1836.
47. Duval, *Early Times in Texas*, 64.
48. Matagorda County Historical Commission, et al., *History of Matagorda County* (Houston: D. Armstrong Co., Inc., 1986), 1:36; Ural Lee Donohoe and Albert C. Horton, Oak Leaves, (November, 1984), IV: 7, 8.
49. White, *Goliad in the Texas Revolution*, 44; Barnard, *Barnard's Journal*, 18, 19; Foote, *Texas and the Texans*, 234; Duval, *Early Times in Texas*, 80; Huson, *Refugio*, 1:324, 336.
50. White, *Goliad in the Texas Revolution*, 45; William Kennedy, *Texas: The Rise, Progress, and Prospects of the Republic of Texas* (Fort Worth: Molyneaux Craftsmen, Inc., 1925), 335.

51. Barnard, *Barnard's Journal*, 20.
52. Foote, *Texas and the Texans*, 238, 239; Dr. Joseph Field, *Three Years in Texas* (Greenfield, Mass.: Justin Jones, 1836), 32; White, *Goliad in the Texas Revolution*, 46.
53. Brown, *History of Texas*, 617-18.
54. Barnard, *Barnard's Journal*, 21, 22; Foote, *Texas and the Texans*, 2:238; Walter P. Webb et al., eds., *The Handbook of Texas* (Austin: The Texas State Historical Association, 1952), 2:594.
55. Foote, *Texas and the Texans*, 239.
56. Foote, *Texas and the Texans*, 240, 241; John J. Linn, *Reminiscences of Fifty Years in Texas*, (New York: D&J Sadlier & Co., 1883), 167; Brown, *History of Texas*, 1:609.
57. Foote, *Texas and the Texans*, 240, 241; Barnard, *Barnard's Journal*, 24.
58. Huson, *Refugio*, 372; Castaneda, *Mexican Side of the Texas Revolution*, 234, 236; Brown, *History of Texas*, 1:618, 619.
59. Foote, *Texas and the Texans*, 243.
60. Huson, *Refugio*, 1:375-376.
61. Duval, *Early Times in Texas*, 89-90, 95-99.
62. Lester Hamilton, *Goliad Survivor* (San Antonio: The Naylor Company, 1971), 3, 8, 9.
63. Barnard, *Barnard's Journal*, 26, 27. After Senora Francisca Alvarez, Angel of Goliad, returned to Matamoros, she continued to help the Americans who were confined there. Her husband abandoned her in Mexico City without funds. Friends who knew of her services gave her warm support.
64. Wharton, *Remember Goliad*, 51.
65. Andrew O'Boyle, "Reminiscences of the Texas Revolution," *Southwest Historical Quarterly*, 13:288-290.
66. Foote, *Texas and the Texans*, 243.
67. Amelia W. Williams, and Eugene C. Barker, *The Writings of Sam Houston 1813-1863* (Austin: The University of Texas Press, 1938), 7:361, 367.
68. Carter, *Masonry in Texas*, 276.

Chapter 7. Fall of the Alamo

1. Louis J. Wortham, *A History of Texas From Wilderness to Common-wealth* (Fort Worth: Wortham-Molyneaux Co., 1924), 3:68. John Henry Brown, *A History of Texas 1685 to 1892* (St. Louis: L.E. Daniell, 1892), 1:480.

2. Walter P. Webb et al., eds., *The Handbook of Texas* (Austin: Texas State Historical Association, 1952), 1:197. Bowie probably was placed in command by the troops, as per custom.
3. Ben Proctor, *The Battle of the Alamo*, (Austin: Texas State Historical Association, 1986), 8, 10, 14.
4. See appendices for list of Gonzales names.
5. Brown, *History of Texas*, 1:566-67.
6. Proctor, *The Battle of the Alamo*, 36.
7. Jose Enrique de la Pena, translated and edited by Carmen Perry, *With Santa Anna in Texas*, (College Station: Texas A&M Press, 1975), 53. Notes on all of the men who died in the Alamo can be found in Bill Groneman, *Alamo Defenders*, (Austin: Eakin Press, 1990).
8. Letter from John Moore to the San Felipe Committee of Safety, October 6, 1835. Archives of Texas, D File, No. 1248; Ethel Zivley Rather, "DeWitt's Colony," *Southwest Historical Quarterly*, 8:157; Eugene C. Barker, ed., *The Austin Papers*, (Austin: The University of Texas Press, 1926), 3:150.
9. Amelia W. Williams and Eugene Barker, eds., *The Writings of Sam Houston, 1813-1863* (Austin: The University of Texas Press, 1938), 1:360, 361.
10. Williams and Barker, *Writings of Sam Houston*, 1:362, 363.
11. Williams and Barker, *Writings of Sam Houston*, 1:311, 365, 366. Houston had a long list of concerns, but Fannin appeared to have an agenda of his own: After failing to relieve the Alamo due to a broken wagon, he later expressed a desire to march upon San Patricio and occupy Copano. It was obvious that Houston and Fannin marched to different drummers; Wortham, *A History of Texas*, 3:234.
12. Williams and Barker, *Writings of Sam Houston*, 1:362. Robinson and his partner, Felix Robertson, were granted the right to settle 800 families on the Brazos River northwest of the Stephen F. Austin grant. Source: Webb, *The Handbook of Texas*, 2:488.
13. Ethel Zivley Rather, "DeWitt's Colony," *Southwest Historical Quarterly*, 8:159, 160, 161. Map 4 shows inner town of Gonzales.
14. Brown, *History of Texas*, 1:590; Wortham, *History of Texas*, 3:237, 2:268 footnote; Henry Stuart Foote, *Texas and the Texans*, (Philadelphia: Thomas Cowperthwait and Co., 1941), 241.
15. A full coverage of the Runaway Scrape will be found in volume two of *Raw Frontier*.
16. Paul E. Lack, *The Texas Revolutionary Experience* (College Station: Texas A&M Press, 1992), 229-231; I.T. Taylor, *The Cavalcade of Jackson County* (San Antonio: The Naylor Company), 79-83.
17. Rather, *Southwest Historical Quarterly*, 8:161.

Chapter 8. Cattle Drives in the Raw Frontier

1. John E. Rouse, *The Criollo, Spanish Cattle in the Americas* (Norman: University of Oklahoma Press, 1977), 23-25.; Kilgore, Dan, "The Spanish Missions and the Origins of the Cattle Industry in Texas." Presented to the Texas State Historical Association in January of 1977 and later published in the *Cattleman* in January, 1983.
2. Nuestra Senora de Espiritu Santo de Zuniga Mission was founded in 1722 on Matagorda Bay, possibly on Garcitas Creek and in 1722 it was moved to a spot on the Guadalupe River somewhere southeast of Victoria. In 1749 it was moved to its final destination on the bank of the San Antonio River near the present town of Goliad. By 1812 the mission's work among the Indians faded when many of their charges deserted to join the Gutierrez-Magee Expedition. It was secularized in 1830. Extensive excavations and renovations started in the 1930s under the old WPA. Today the restored mission is operated by the State Park System. (Webb, Walter Prescott, et al, *Handbook of Texas*, Austin: Texas State Historical Association), 2:293
3. Carlos Edward Castaneda, *Our Catholic Heritage, 1519-1936* (Austin: Von Boeckmann-Jones Co., 1936), 5:24, 29, 187-89.
4. Admiral A.B.J. Hammett, *The Empresario* (Waco: Texian Press, 1973), 87.
5. Herbert Eugene Bolton, *Texas in the Middle Eighteenth Century* (Austin: University of Texas Press, 1970), 382.
6. Walter Prescott Webb, *The Great Plains* (New York: Grosset & Dunlap, 1931), 208-09.
7. Keith Guthrie, *History of San Patricio County* (Austin: Nortex Publishers, 1986), 54.
8. Keith Guthrie, *Texas Forgotten Ports, vol. 3*, (Austin: Eakin Press, 1995), 139; *Beaumont Journal*, March 19, 1927.
9. Mrs. I. C. Madry, *History of Bee County* (Beeville: Beeville Publishing Co., 1939), 10.
10. *Columbia Telegraph*, December 17, 1836.
11. *Corpus Christi Star*, Saturday, February 10, 1849.
12. Marcellus filed on 640 acres using, land warrant No. 562, issued September 27, 1838 to his father, Col. Amasa Turner.
13. Boethel, Paul C., *The Gentleman From Lavaca*, (Austin: Von Boeckmann-Jones, 1963), 94-95; "Marcellus Turner to Col. A. Turner, April 6, 1856"; Copies of Turner Letters in possession of Keith Guthrie; Original letters now in Barker History Center, Austin. (Rugeley Collection).
14. Paul C. Boethel, *The Gentleman From Lavaca*, 88.

15. *State of Texas vs. H.H. Hunter et al.* No. 289, Criminal Docket, District Court of San Patricio County, Tex., vol. A-212.`

16. This was a practice of taking cattle for use by Confederate forces without permission of the owner. General John Magruder issued the order. Judge Wm. Gable was delegated by stock raisers of Oakville to visit the headquarters of General E. Kirby Smith to try and get a change in the order to impress cattle without restriction. Walker admitted that the complaint was just but evidently no relief was granted.

17. *The Ranchero*, November 7, 1864. Note: This issue of *The Ranchero* was published in Santa Margarita, a community across the river from San Patricio, due to the threatening Yankee fleet in Nueces Bay.

18. *Nueces Valley*, October 24, 1857. (Deponent: One who gives evidence.).

19. Approximately 300,000 hides were shipped from Rockport and Corpus Christi in 1872. (*Corpus Christi Gazette*, February 7, 1874).

20. J. Frank Dobie, *A Vaquero of the Brush Country* (Austin: University of Texas Press, 1929), 24.

21. Ron Tyler, et al., eds., *New Handbook of Texas* (Austin: Texas State Historical Association, 1996), 5:194.

22. Mitchell Family History, Papers in possession of Mary Catherine Dickey, Lolita, Texas; and Keith Guthrie, *Historic Matagorda County*, 178-79.

23. Guthrie, *Texas Forgotten Ports*, 93.

24. Ibid., 43.

25. Chris Emmett, (Norman: University of Oklahoma Press, 1953), 31.

26. Guthrie, *History of San Patricio County*, 56, 57. When the company started in 1871 they had in excess of 371,000 acres of land in Aransas, San Patricio, Live Oak, and Goliad counties. It was reorganized in 1879, with the Mathis partners pulling out, cutting the acreage to about 261,000. It was then known as the Coleman-Fulton Pasture Company.

27. Guthrie, *Texas Forgotten Ports*, 43.

28. Brownson Malsch, *Indianola, the Mother of West Texas* (Austin: State House Press, 1988,), 37, 56, 189; Calhoun County Historical Committee, *Indianola Scrap Book* (Austin: Jenkins Publishing Co, 1974), 24.

29. J. Marvin Hunter, *The Trail Drivers of Texas* (New York: Argosy-Antiquarian Ltd., 1963,) 807-09; "The Rachals of White Point," paper compiled from family interviews by Rachal Bluntzer Hebert in cooperation with Betty Gay Ash, a Rachal descendant. Copies in the Rachal family and in the possession of Keith Guthrie.

30. Ibid., 963.

31. United States Agriculture Census, 1880, 3:975.
32. Dobie, *A Vaquero of the Brush Country*, 23.
33. Hunter, *The Trail Drivers of Texas*, 575.
34. Ibid., 295-99.
35. Ibid., 403.
36. A. Ray Stephens, *The Taft Ranch* (Austin: University of Texas Press), 50.
37. Hunter, *The Trail Drivers of Texas*, 589.
38. Ibid., 635-36.
39. Ibid., 685.
40. Cattle who could not keep up with the herd.
41. Hunter, *The Trail Drivers of Texas*, 293-294.
42. Ibid., 294-95.
43. Ibid., 455-57.
44. Interview on March 18, 1996 with Mrs. Charlotte Nichols at her home in Kenedy. The Butlers came to Karnes County in 1852 and the Nichols in 1854. Her husband was W. G. "Bill" Butler's grandson. She is considered an authority on Butler history.
45. Hunter, *The Trail Drivers of Texas*, 480-85, 715-18; Charlotte Nichols Interview.
46. Charlotte Nichols Interview.
47. The Battle of Arkansas Post, January 1, 1863. Letter written by Josephine Mills in Arkansas to her friend Lizzie Choate in Karnes County, dated 2-5-1863. Letter in possession of Mrs. Nichols; copy Keith Guthrie.
48. Charlotte Nichols Interview.
49. Webb, et al., eds., *Handbook of Texas*, 3:360.
50. Hunter, Trail Drivers of Texas, 183-86.
51. Ibid., 923.
52. Personal Interview with Mrs. Mary Catherine Dickey August 9, 1996; Mitchell family papers, 31 (in possession of Mrs. Dickey and author.)
53. Guthrie, *Texas Forgotten Ports*, 197-98.
54. Burns, J. C., *Sketch of My Life*, (Privately printed, copies in family: Mrs. Blair James Carey, Cuero), 8; Tyler et al., eds., *New Handbook of Texas*, 4:176.
55. Burns, *Sketch of My life*, 1, 2.
56. Ibid., 517.
57. Ibid., 397.
58. Ibid., 691.
59. *Historical and Biographical Record of Cattle Industry and Cattlemen of Texas*, Introduction by J. Frank Dobie, (New York: Antiquarian Press, Ltd., 1959). 607-08, 616; Hunter, *Trail Drivers of Texas*, 730-34.
60. Hunter, *Trail Drivers of Texas*, 426-33.

Chapter 9. The Cart Road and the Cart War

1. Depending on the locality, the old road was also known as the Goliad Road, American Freight Road, Old Freighter's Road, Mexican Cart Trail, or First Texas Road.
2. Charles S. Potts, *Railroad Transportation in Texas* (Austin: University of Texas, 1909), 17-19.
3. In 1840 the Victoria County Commissioners approved rates for a municipal ferry which was replaced partly with a toll bridge in 1851. The Kemper Bluffs and White ferries also offered a means to cross the river.
4. El Fuerte del Cibolo was built by the Spanish to protect ranches between the San Antonio River and the Cibolo Creek sometime in the early 1700s. In 1774 the fort was strengthened with troops drawn from Los Adaes, La Bahia, and the Rio Grande (Dunn, William Edward, "Apache Relations in Texas 1717-1750," *Southwestern Historical Quarterly*, 14:198-274). It was to serve as a defense point between La Bahia and San Antonio. It was abandoned a few years later.
5. *San Antonio Express*, June 5, 1936.
6. Hedwig Krell Didear, *Helena of Karnes County and Old Helena* (Austin: Jenkins Publishing Co., 1969), 18, 19.
7. Didear, *Helena of Karnes County and Old Helena*, 16; L. W. Newton and H. P. Campbell, *Texas Yesterday and Today* (Dallas: Turner Publishing Co., 1949), 41.
8. Louis J. Wortham, *History of Texas* (New York: World Co., 1924), 4:231; Didear, *Helena of Karnes County and Old Helena*, 19; Mrs. Anna J. Pennybacker, *New History of Texas*, (Palestine: Percy V. Pennybacker, 1885), 257; Alice Freeman Fluth, "Indianola Early Gateway to Texas," (Master's thesis, St. Mary's University of San Antonio, 1939), 41.
9. Arnold DeLeon, *They Called Them Greasers* (Austin: University of Texas Press, 1983), 82.
10. Irene Hohmann Fredrichs, *History of Goliad*, (Victoria: Regal Printers, 1961), 33-34. The Hanging Tree still provides shade for the courthouse square and is marked with an historical marker.
11. Wortham, *History of Texas*, 4:232.
12. Didear, *Helena of Karnes County and Old Helena*, 18-21; Linn, John J., *Reminiscences of Fifty Years in Texas* (Austin: State House Press, 1986), 253; Bancroft, Hubert Howe, *History of the North Mexican States and Texas*, 1531-1899, (New York: McCraw Hill Book Company, 1967), 2:219.
13. Wortham, *History of Texas*, 4:232.
14. Pennybacker, *New History of Texas*, 256-57.

15. Homer S. Thrall, *Pictorial History of Texas* (New York: Thompson Co., 1879), 772-73.

Appendices

1. John Henry Brown, *History of Texas from 1685 to 1802* (St. Louis: L. E. Daniell, 1892), 1:431-435. This was not the first declaration of independence. Col. John Wharton declined appointment as a commissioner to the United States, stating, in part: "I believe that under any declaration short of absolute independence, we will receive no efficient or permanent aid or pecuniary assistance from the United States." In Nacogdoches on November 15 twenty-one members of the committee of safety passed a strong resolution in favor of independence. In Brazoria on December 15 a resolution was adopted favoring a formal declaration of independence (Wharton was a member of this committee). A similar meeting was held in Columbia on December 25 at which time the committee approved a resolution in favor of independence.

BIBLIOGRAPHY

Archival Material

Bexar Archives (Texas A&M-Corpus Christi Library), Angel Navarro to Alcalde of Goliad, Sept. 21, 1835, reel 1666, frames 784-85; Guadalupe de los Santos to Angel Navarro, Sept. 25, 1835, reel 1666, frame 808.

"Gonzales, The Lexington of Texas," vertical file Gonzales Public Library.

Letter from John Moore to the San Felipe Committee of Safety, October 6, 1835, Archives of Texas, D file, No. 1248.

Memorial/Petitions (San Patricio seeking permission to operate under pre-revolution frame work), Texas State Archives.

Books

Austin, Stephen F. *Austin Papers,* Austin: University of Texas Press, 1927.

Barker, Eugene C. ed., *The Austin Papers,* 3 vols., Austin: University of Texas Press, 1926.

Barnard, Dr. J.H. *Dr. J.H. Barnard's Journal.* Printed by *Goliad Advance, The Journal* was first published in the *Goliad Guard* in 1883 and reprinted in 1912 by the *Goliad Advance,* J.A. White editor. Reprinted 1965 and 1988.

Binkley, William Campbell. *The Expansionist Movement in Texas, 1836-1850,* Berkley, Calif.: University of California Press, 1925.

———. *Official Correspondence of the Texas Revolution, 1835-1836,* New York: D. Appleton-Century Co., 1936.

Boddie, Mary Delaney. *Thunder on the Brazos,* Dallas: Taylor Publishing Co., 1978.

Bradfield, Jane. *Rx Take One Cannon,* Shiner: Patrick J. Wagner Research and Publishing Co., 1981.

Brown, John Henry. *History of Texas From 1685 to 1892*, St. Louis: L.E. Daniell, 1892.

———. *Life and Times of Henry Smith*, Austin: Steck Company, 1935.

Castaneda, Carlos E. *The Mexican side of the Texan Revolution*, Austin: Graphic Ideas, Inc.,1970.

Carter, James David. *Education and Masonry in Texas to 1846*, Waco: Committee on Masonic Education and Service for the Grand Lodge of Texas, A.F. and A.M, 1963

Deaton, Charles. *Texas Postal History Handbook*, Privately printed, 1991.

Dobie, J. Frank. *Coronado's Children*, Austin: University of Texas Press, 1981.

Duval, John C. Edited by Mabel Major and Rebecca W. Smith. *Early Times in Texas*, Lincoln: University of Nebraska Press, 1986.

Field, Dr. Joseph. *Three Years in Texas*, Greenfield, Mass.; Justin Jones, 1836.

Filisola, Don Vicente, translated by Wallace Woolsey. *Memoirs for the History of the War in Texas*, 2 vols., Austin: Eakin Press, 1985, 2 Vols.

Foote, Henry Stuart. *Texas and the Texans*, Philadelphia: Thomas, Cowperthwait & Co., 1841.

Gammel, H.P. *Laws of Texas, 1822-1897*, 10 vols., Austin: The Gammel Book Company, 1898.

Grimes, Roy. *300 Years in Victoria County*, Victoria: Victoria Advocate Publishing Co., 1985

Guthrie, Keith. *Texas Forgotten Ports*, 3 vols., Austin: Eakin Press, 1988, 1993 Vols. I, II.

———. *History of San Patricio County*, Austin, Nortex Publishers, 1986.

Hamilton, Lester. *Goliad Survivor*, San Antonio: The Naylor Company, 1971.

Hebert, Rachel Bluntzer. *The Forgotten Colony*, Burnet: Eakin Press, 1981.

Henson, Margaret Swett. *Juan Davis Bradburn*, College Station: Texas A&M University Press, 1982.

Hicks, John. *The Federal Union*, Boston: Houghton Miffin Company, 1937.

Huson, Hobart, *Refugio, A Comprehensive History of Refugio County From Aboriginal Times to 1953*, 2 vols., Houston: Guardsman Publishing Company, 1953.

———. *Captain Philip Dimmitt's Commandancy of Goliad 1835-1836*, Austin: Von Boeckmann-Jones Co., 1974.

Jenkins, John H., ed., *The Papers of the Texas Revolution*, Austin: Presidial Press, 1973.

Johnson, Frank W. *Texas and Texans*, Chicago and New York: The American Historical Society, edited and brought up to date by Eugene C. Barker with assistance of Ernest Wm. Winkler, 1916.

Kennedy, William. *Rise, Progress, and Prospects of the Republic of Texas*, Fort Worth: Molyneaux Craftsmen, Inc., 1925.

————. *Texas, Its Geography, Natural History and Topography*, New York: Benjamin & Young, 1844.

Kilman, Ed, *Cannibal Coast*, San Antonio: The Naylor Company, 1959.

Lack, Paul D. *The Texas Revolutionary Experience*, College Station: Texas A&M Press, 1992.

Laour, Lucian Knight. *Georgia's Bi-Centennial Memoirs and Memories*, Privately printed by author and dedicated to Hon. Cordell Hull, a friend of the author, 1933.

Linn, John J. *Reminiscences of Fifty Years in Texas*, Austin: State House Press, 1986.

Matagorda County Historical Commission, 3 vols., *Historic Matagorda County*, Houston: D. Armstrong Co., Inc., 1986.

Newton, Lewis W. and Herbert Gambrell. *A Social and Political History of Texas*, Dallas: Southwest Press, 1932.

Oberste, William H. *Remember Goliad*, Austin: Von Boeckmann-Jones, 1949.

Pena, Jose Enrique de la. *With Santa Anna in Texas*, College Station: Texas A&M University Press, 1975.

Proctor, Ben. *The Battle of the Alamo*, Austin: Texas State Historical Association, 1986.

Rouse, John E. *The Cariollo, Spanish Cattle in the Americas*, Norman: University of Oklahoma Press, 1977.

Smither, Harriet, ed. *The Papers of Mirabeau Lamar*, Austin: Von Boeckmann-Jones Co., 1927.

Taylor, I.T. *The Cavalcade of Jackson County*, San Antonio: The Naylor Company, 1938.

Taylor, Paul Schuster. *An American-Mexican Frontier, Nueces County, Texas*, New York: Russell & Russell, 1934.

Thonhoff, Robert H. *El Fuerte Del Cibolo, Sentinel of the Bexar-La Bahia Ranches*, Austin: Eakin Press, 1992.

Webb, Walter Prescott, et al. *The Handbook of Texas*, 3 vols., Austin: Texas State Historical Association, 1952.

Wharton, Clarence R. *Texas, Under Many Flags*, Chicago/New York: American Historical Society, 1939.

————. *Remember Goliad*, Glorieta, N.M.: The Rio Grande Press, Inc., 1931.

White, Nell. *Goliad in the Texas Revolution*, Privately printed in 1988 by Nell White Hargreaves (Book taken from Miss White's masters thesis at the University of Houston in 1941.

Williams, Amelia and Eugene Barker, editors. *Writings of Sam Houston, 1813-1863*, Austin: The University of Texas Press, 1938.

Wortham, Louis J. *A History of Texas From Wilderness to Commonwealth,* 2 vols., Fort Worth: Wortham-Molyneaux Co., 1950.

Yoakum, H. *History of Texas,* New York: Redfield, 1856.

Newspapers

Bee Picayune, "Memories of Old Bee County, History of Casa Blanca" by Camp Ezell (Reprinted from an article in the *San Antonio Express,* Dec. 13, 1931. The series ran for five weeks in May of 1950.)

Gonzales Inquirer, "Outstanding Dates in DeWitt Colony," undated in vertical file of Gonzales Public Library.

Houston Telegraph and Register, January 9, 1836.

Kilgore, Dan "Texans Ousted Mexicans From Nueces County Fort," *Corpus Christi Caller-Times,* January 18, 1959.

San Antonio Express, "Lagarto Near Vanishing Point . . .," By Dudley Dobie, November 18, 1934, section D, 1.

Series of articles by John Norris, confidant of Mrs. Wallis Wade for over 30 years, that appeared in the *Mathis News* in July and August of 1985. Mrs. Wade died in 1973. The abstract is now in the John Connor Museum, Kingsville, Tex.

Telegraph and Register, Saturday, October, 1835 (Published in San Felipe).

Pamphlets, Speeches, and Interviews

Kilgore, D.E. *Nueces County, Texas 1750-1800, A Bicentennial Memoir,* Corpus Christi: Friends of the Corpus Christi Museum, 1975.

Periodicals and Journals

Davenport, Harbert, "Captain Jesus Cuellar, Texas Cavalry, Otherwise known as *Comanche,*" *Southwestern Historical Quarterly,* 63:56-62.

Donohoe, Ural Lee and Albert C. Norton, *Oak Leaves,* November 1984, Publication of the Orange County Historical Society, located in Orange, Tex., public library.

Howren, Alleine, "Causes and Origin of the Decree of April 6, 1830," *Southwestern Historical Quarterly,* 16:415.

Letter of Librarian Edward S. Holden, of U.S. Military Academy, to Dr. C.W. Raines, State Librarian, Austin, Tex., *Southwestern Historical Quarterly,* 7:320.

O'Boyle, Andrew, "Reminiscences of the Texas Revolution," *Southwestern Historical Quarterly,* 20:121.

"Order to Smith, et al.," October 12, 1835, "Austin's Order Book," *Southwestern Historical Quarterly,* 16:95-100..

Rather, Ethel Zivley, "DeWitt's Colony," *The Quarterly, Texas State Historical Association,* Vol. 8:95-199, Oct. 1904.

Vertical file, Gonzales Public Library: "Gonzales was Featured by Progressive Farmer," Progressive Farmer, 1953.

Public Records

Lucio Moya et al. vs O'Connor, Estates of J.M. O'Brien and Nannie Hart O'Brien, 36th Judicial District, Bee County, May 16, 1975, No. 13:758.

San Patricio County Census of 1850.

Theses

Dixon, Frederick Kent, "A History of Gonzales County in the Nineteenth Century," Master of Arts Thesis, Austin: University of Texas, 1964.

Unpublished Material

Archaeological Investigations at Fort Lipantitlan, December 1988 by James E. Warren with Skip Kennedy and Nancy Beaman (earlier report was done in 1974 by J. Daviding, Archaeological Report 16, Texas Parks and Wildlife Department).

Kilgore, D.E., "Spanish and Mexican Land Grants," paper prepared after authoring *Nueces County, Texas 1750-1800, A Bicentennial Memoir,* (Corpus Christi: Friends of the Corpus Christi Museum), December 1975.

INDEX

89421